What Happened When The Dish Ran Away With The Spoon?

(Memoirs of a Petsitter)

By Margaret L Streitenberger

Illustrated by Jim Arnold

Printed by Speedway Press, Oswego, New York

First book in the Hey Diddle Diddle Series

Publisher's Cataloging-In-Publication Data

Streitenberger, Margaret, 1939-
What Happened When the Dish Ran Away With the Spoon
(Memoirs of a Pet sitter) / Margaret Streitenberger and Jim
Arnold

    p.cm.
ISBN 978-0-9832626-0-2
    1. Entrepreneurship-pet sitting. 2. Animal stories
    I. Streitenberger, Margaret, 2010- II. Title.

This book is dedicated to the memory of the pets in our book who have passed on and their guardians who are saddened by the loss of their companions. The pets are waiting, now without pain or care, until the day they are reunited with their guardians, and they walk across the rainbow bridge together.

Acknowledgments

There are so many people and animals that have helped make me a storyteller who loves animals. I want to especially thank the pets and their guardians who provided me with experiences and lessons through my pet-sitting business to share with you the readers. Many of the guardians enjoyed the reports and encouraged me to write more.

I wish to thank my many friends who urged me on to create this book especially: Dr. Mary Bochino-Kerker, DVM who was my professional resource on animals and who first suggested that I ask Jim Arnold to be my illustrator; Rose Allen who never stopped telling me to "get it done"; Pat O'Neil who advised me on writing and reviewed my many attempts to write this book.

I feel so lucky to have connected with Jim Arnold, many years younger than I, but willing to partner his unique artistic skills and love of animals with my storytelling. This has been a grand adventure and partnership.

Finally, I wish to thank Maggie Majlaton who accepted the task of "shepherding Jim and I through this process" to print. She re-energized our focus and has become mentor, editor, web-master and whatever else we need as we emerge in our partnership.

Margaret (Tumbleweed) Streitenberger, Author

I've got to thank my parents, for without their boundless love, support, and encouragement I never could have come so far with my art or even have put this book together. I'm grateful also to have somehow wound up working with Margaret Streitenberger, a hero and mentor, who has so much to share with everyone. Thank you to friends and family who have encouraged me along the way as well. I am truly blessed.

Jim Arnold, Artist

CONTENTS
INTRODUCTION

Hey Diddle Diddle
The Cat and the Fiddle
The Cow jumped over the Moon

The Little Dog Laughed
To see such fun
While the Dish Ran Away with the Spoon

Nursery Rhymes were often written as political satire with word caricatures of people and situations. As I was setting up my pet sitting business, I selected one of my favorite rhymes as representative and descriptive of my service.

Did the Dish run away with the Spoon or "to spoon"? No Matter! Dish and Spoon will represent the caregivers and daily nurturers of the family which would include the pets.

When the dish and spoon take time off to travel for pleasure and/ or business, frequently they are unable to take their pets with them. Substitute caregivers are available at kennels, pet day camps, and various other options outside of the home. However, I joined the growing number of pet sitters who provide the option of leaving the pets in the familiar surroundings of their own homes where they are visited according to their regular routines.

My service was to keep the kitties fiddling and doggies laughing. So I, as the cow, might not jump over the moon but through all the hoops needed to entertain, nourish and provide companionship for those left at home while the rest of the family roamed.

I selected "Hey Diddle Diddle" as the name of my pet sitting service. I spent many wonderful hours being the one entertained as well as nourished and loved in the companionship of animals who learned love from their guardians. Unlike people who work with discarded and abused animals and are frequently overwhelmed by the cruel side of humans, I worked with animals that were all well loved and I experienced the greatness of human nature.

The animals greeted me with trust because their guardians did the same. I felt stabilized by the contact with these animals. I was humbled by the owners trust in allowing me into their homes to care for their precious pets. With their approval, I want to share some stories of these encounters and the lessons taught to me by the pets who have been my best teachers.

Did you ever wonder what happens when you're not home? Well read on and find out how the cat fiddles and the dog laughs and the pet sitter jumps over the moon while the dish is away with the spoon!!

1. Getting Started

Helping a Friend

A veterinarian friend needed a vacation. However she would be traveling with the person she usually trusted to care for her pets and she was hesitant to leave her pets with someone else. Since she had been encouraging me to follow my dream of starting a pet sitting business as my retirement project, I convinced her to let me take care of her pets. Even so, she was not really sure that I could handle J.E.B.

J.E.B. was a large dog and I do mean LARGE, being of "mixed heritage" which definitely included German Shepherd (and probably wolf). As a puppy, it had even been hard for my vet friend to predict the humongous body that J.E.B. grew into. He was well trained but devoted to and protective of his owner. His open crate was just inside the back door. When entering the closed in back porch, his bark from the other side of the kitchen door was enough to scare most people away. It was his way of saying, "Do not enter here!" If you were feeling really brave and proceeded to knock on the door, it took tremendous courage to face his size even with his guardian holding him back firmly as he growled protectively. J.E.B. was used to walking three times a day on a mowed path that circled a large field which was surrounded by woods. He loved skunks which could present a stinky problem for me, so I paid attention where the large container of Listerine was kept. Because J.E.B. was so large and very muscular, he could easily drag me or get away

from me if he were startled by deer, a coyote or even rabbits coming from the woods. I practiced walking him with his guardian close at hand.

On my first visit without the guardian present, I filled my pockets with milk bones, put on my sturdy mountain climbing shoes, tucked a brush in my pocket, put J.E.B.'s leash on, and took a good strong hold of the lead. As we started out the door for our first walk I said, "J.E.B.! Remember! I am an old woman unlike your owner and I can't walk very fast."

J.E.B. totally understood. He gently led the way. Every so often he would stop and look back at me to make sure I was okay. When we got half way around the circle, I asked him to stop. He did! I brushed his thick coat for a while and we watched his hair blow away in the breeze. Then, of course, he was rewarded with a couple of milk bones. When we arrived back at the house, J.E.B. jumped into the chair on the back porch. After closing the porch door, I unfastened his lead and gave him another reward. He loved his milk bones, so I was careful of my fingers as I gave him his treats.

Sometimes, the last part of the walk got a little trickier for me. J.E.B. would anticipate the treat and/or meals waiting for him and begin to speed up as we neared the house. His dry food was measured out to keep his weight in control because of his arthritic hips. He loved to take his pills for those arthritic hips because the pills would be wrapped in cream cheese. Catching "baby carrots" as I tossed them to him was delightful play. If he missed one, I apologized since I was a poor tosser and I didn't want to undermine his confidence as a catcher. After our regular routine, J.E.B. would retire to his crate and wait for me to leave. He knew and expected that I would give him one more dog treat as I passed his crate which was right at the back door.

In the same house was a <u>long-haired gray and white cat named **Derry**.</u> That's short for Derelict since he had been found as an injured dehydrated kitten, dying behind the medical delivery box at the veterinary clinic. He was discovered just in time! I knew Derry was in the house because his litter pans had been used. He liked two pans: one to do his "duty" in and the other to walk across to keep his feet clean. Also, some of his food would have been eaten. His food dish was always placed in a small crate so that he could get into it but J.E.B. could not even get his nose in.

Another sign of Derry's presence: J.E.B.'s water dish would be empty. His water dish had to be placed in a long flat pan because Derry liked to use his paws to scoop out the water. The long pan kept it from going all over the kitchen floor.

Derry was one of those cats who like to see but not be seen. I found one of his hiding places behind an end table by the couch. After assigned tasks were finished, I would sit on the couch for awhile, sometimes with the TV on, to get him comfortable with my scent and presence. However, J.E.B. would walk in from his crate and look at me as if to say, "Aren't you leaving yet? I'm waiting for my treat." I would invite him to lie down next to me. But he would just go back to his crate and wait.

I was encouraged by these two and their warm response to me and felt ready to pursue my dream. I learned from J.E.B. that he understood what I said and that he would accommodate my age. I learned from both J.E.B. and Derry that basically they were in charge and would remind me of their needs and wants.

I realized that the animals would help me if they could just stay at home in their familiar surroundings while the family was away.

Spreading the Word

Hey Diddle Diddle, Pet and House sitting service! I turned my favorite nursery rhyme into the name of my new business.

I made up my own business cards and started handing them out to known pet owners. Two houses north of my home on Route

48 about a mile north of Fulton, NY lived a family whose teenage children had knocked on my door whenever they were raising money for band trips. I knew they had a couple of dogs, so I knocked on their door this time. I gave them my card and explained my new business. They expressed willingness to support my effort, but had already planned to take their two dogs and cat with them as they delivered their daughter to college in Maine and then vacationed for a couple weeks in New England. However, they would really be happy if I could take care of their turtle named Rocky.

Rocky was a Red-Eared Slider. His back (shell/house) was probably about 3 inches in diameter. He lived in an aquarium with large rocks that he could climb onto allowing him to get out of the water and bask under the heat of the hood light. It sounded like a simple task: Drop a few pieces of food into the tank twice a day. The only

thing that could cause a problem would be the loss of electricity in a storm, requiring restarting of the pump. It would not restart automatically when the electricity kicked back on. The pump was essential to the turtle's health since it kept the water fresh and filtered. Sounded simple enough!!

Rocky and I greeted each other twice a day. He seemed to sense my arrival. I dropped his food into the tank and then, per directions, I would put my finger to the glass indicating where the food had floated to the side. He played the game and let me direct him to his food.

He scared me once when I didn't see him in the tank and thought he might have gotten out. When I moved the hood to take a closer look, I heard a splash as he dropped into the water. He probably had climbed from his rock trying to reach the "sun". Other than that, our routine was fairly uneventful.

When I took this job I explained to the family that I was already committed for one day during the two week assignment to drive a couple of Syracuse youth to school in Brooklyn. The guardians were okay with feeding Rocky earlier that day and assured me, that even if I missed his feeding just one night, Rocky should be fine. As it happened, one of the students ran into a problem because the school had entered her social security number incorrectly in their system. It took longer than expected to work through the school's "tangled web" in order to get the student accepted and into her residence.

Driving back to Syracuse in the dark with a tearful mother crying over the "loss" of her daughter left behind at school, a terrible thunderstorm overwhelmed us at Scranton, Pennsylvania. In the pouring rain, with streaks of lightening flashing around us, all I could think of was Rocky and the pump in his tank. Would he survive until I could get his pump restarted?

I reached my own driveway around midnight. There were signs that it had rained here too. I had hoped the storm would remain south of upstate New York. Tired and tripping over my own feet, I hurried over to Rocky's house. I let myself into the house and worried all the way up the steps imagining Rocky floating on his back in the water!

What a Relief! The tank was lit up and the pump was pumping away. Rocky was sitting in the light on his rock waiting for his dinner.

It was great getting to know an unfamiliar animal. I also learned that like us, the animals can tolerate a delay in a meal as long as they eventually get it.

Developing a Report Card

The next step was to develop the necessary business forms and description of expected routines for pet sitting. My insurance agent suggested bonding and I needed customers to sign forms giving me the permission to enter their homes.

A friend from work was taking his daughter on a weekend trip. He hired me to take care of his dog and cat.

Josh was a Schipperke. I was grateful for the internet where I could quickly get information on unfamiliar breeds. It seems that the sturdy little black dog, the Schipperke, was a "sea dog". He was a great companion on barges. While I had been totally unfamiliar with this breed and Josh was a delightful first, I have since met and pet-sat several Schipperkes.

His master/guardian agreed on a routine for his walks and feeding schedule.

When I arrived for the first visit without the family present, Josh was restless and uneasy. All the time, he watched the door for the return of his family. So I pulled out a book that I had brought along, settled comfortably on the couch, and proceeded to read. Josh sat watching me for a while. Then, he laid at my feet for a short time. Finally, he came up on the couch and cuddled up next to me. We made a lot of progress in the first visit!

I am not a trainer. I am not a groomer or an expert on pet nutrition. But I found that I had a low vibration that calmed the pets in the absence of their families. So, I built this "quiet time/cuddle time" into my service, making sure that I planned time to just be there with them and supply the human element that had left with the family.

Josh had a companion cat named Spooky. **Spooky** was an "in and out" cat. My own cats, being mostly strays and living near a busy highway, had to agree to stay inside if they wanted in from the cold. Since winters are rough in Upstate New York, they were very happy to become "inside cats". However, I learned to adjust to customers' desires and routines. Even though I was uncomfortable with the possibility of losing someone else's pet. Spooky was used to following Josh down the street when he took his daily walks. Luckily, he followed us back and was in the house when I left.

Part of my service was to leave a report that families would find on their arrival home. I did request a call letting me know that they had arrived home safely because I felt responsible for their pets until I knew the family was back to care for them.

Following is the first report card in my new role as a Tattle-Tale: one who tells tales on the tails' activities.

Josh:

Josh did a great job of watering all of the trees on your side of the street.
I was a little concerned because he didn't eat much or do any "poop" on Saturday. He seemed to keep watching for you. So I spent a half hour reading and just sitting quietly petting him when he came to sit with me. When I came back on Sunday morning, he greeted me warmly. We had a nice walk and a good "duty". He had eaten all the food left out and looked for more.
He seemed settled and at ease when I left Sunday.

Spooky:

Spooky was in when I arrived Friday Night. He ate well of his own and Josh's food.
He didn't seem to make any attempt to go outside Saturday. He watched from behind a chair while I sat and read and petted Josh. He did come up to me to be petted a couple of times.
Sunday morning, he was ready to go out when Josh and I went for the regular morning walk. He followed along. We took a little extra long walk. The air was great and they both seemed to be enjoying the "watering" of trees and shrubs. Spooky disappeared for a while after chasing a squirrel and didn't come in when Josh did. However, he was at the door when I was ready to leave. He came in, went for the food, and was eating noisily when I left.

House Notes: When I arrived on Friday P.M., the landlord was fixing some plumbing in the bathroom. He left before I did, saying that he would return to fix the knob on the inner door. He must have come back later because in the morning the knob had been changed and there was some black dust on the floor near the door.

I had decided to create the House Notes section to alert the family to anything noteworthy (or broken) during their absence. Also, to protect my bonding, I made note of anyone besides myself that I knew was in the house during the family's absence. In this case, the entry of the landlord was unexpected by the family. It turned out that he had installed illegal equipment in the home. This written witness to his presence provided proof to the family in their legal procedures. So this definitely confirmed the House Notes as an important piece of the service that I provided.

Taking care of pets in their own home provided the security to owners that their homes appeared to be occupied while the family was away. Mail and Newspapers could still be delivered and brought inside daily. If there was storm damage etc. it could be reported immediately to the family when it happened and not just found on their return. If they wished, they could even get the repairs started before their return.

Besides bonding, I also joined NAPPS (The National Association of Professional Pet Sitters) to help professionalize my services.

With Name Selected, DBA filed, business cards and word of mouth providing advertisement of the service, business forms in place, and gas in the car we are now ready for the tale to begin!

2. Some Stayed Home
While the Dish Ran Away With the Spoon
Tails and Tales from the Winter of 2001

Meet the Tails

This is an introduction to the pets that I cared for while their families traveled elsewhere. Due to good friends and fellow employees, my first business quarter flourished with many requests for service. The pets are listed in the order of their appearance into my life and my pet sitting practice. I provided human companionship in their homes while the guardians were away. The pets returned love, entertainment and some of the best life lessons.

Moon and Rosie, companion felines, shared a home in North Fulton. Entrance used was ground floor basement entered from and level with the driveway. There was a counter just inside the door and an open stairway into the kitchen. The litter pan was in the basement.

Moon was a black short-haired male well muscled from his hunts in the wetland area nearby, referred to as "the swamp". He definitely loved being outside, sometimes staying out over night. The door to an outside portico was to be left ajar so he could find shelter in bad weather. Inside, he preferred sleeping on a kitchen chair under the table.

Rosie, an older feline, was a gray, short- haired female tiger. She went outside for shorter periods and stayed near the house, often sitting on the low concrete wall outside by the back door. Inside, Rosie preferred the center of the bed for her long naps.

Molly, Emmy Lou, Flopsy and Rocky were my neighbors who lived two houses up the road on Route 48 north of Fulton. The dogs, Molly and Emmy, were trained to run off lead outside. They knew to stay in the back yard that ran to the Oswego River and to avoid the front yard that faced the busy highway. They were crate trained and were happy to go there to eat, sleep and cool down or take a break. The crates were placed in a dry safe place in the basement. The terminology they were trained to respond to included:

Crate: the inside feeding and sleeping station

Kennel: the outside run

Get Busy: to go potty

Dead: Molly was to drop the ball (She had been trained for hunting to retrieve dead fowl.)

Cookie: milk bone or dog biscuits. This word is understood in both of our languages

Molly was a chocolate Labrador Retriever with endless energy. She will be referred to as **Molly Brown** in order to identify her as separate from the later Molly to enter my clientele.

Emmy Lou was a small black Cocker Spaniel. She was older and beginning to have some hearing problems.

Flopsy was a long-haired large Maine Coon female feline. She preferred to be upstairs and away from the dogs. She was easily stressed which led to vomiting. Her water bowl was kept by the bathroom upstairs.

Rocky was a Red-Eared Slider turtle. He spent 24/7 in a fish tank provided with a large rock to sit on at times and bask in the light in the hood. His residence was located on the second floor in the room across from the bathroom.

Abdual, Akeem, Been Kitty, Harry, Iggy, NoNo Baby, Norman, Sebastian, Shirley Louise (a.k.a. Mama) were all rescued cats and shared a home with several rescued dogs. When the dogs traveled with their guardians, I was trusted to watch the kitties. Their home was located on Route 48 just south of Minetto. A back room was separated from the kitchen by a screen door. Like in a British drama, there was an upstairs kitty, downstairs kitties and back room kitties. Litter boxes and dry food dispensers were placed in all three areas. The litter boxes all had hoods that made it impossible for the dogs to get at cat feces. One open pan was kept in the back room because Harry couldn't climb into the others.

Abdual a rescued feral kitty always remained shy with most humans and would hide under one of the beds upstairs. I was told that I would probably not see her during my time there and warned that she used her claws.

Akeem was a sister to Abdual, also a rescued feral kitty. She had short black hair with white markings and was a great huntress. She was in the back room and represented death to all intruding mice or voles.

Harry was rescued after a bad injury on the road. He had a sweet personality in spite of his crippled walk which made it hard to climb into the big litter pans. He lives in the back room where accidents are all forgivable. He was a long haired orange male with white markings. He tended to get more mats than most cats and had runny eyes.

Sebastian was an ancient short haired black female. She was the only one allowed to go outside because she didn't go anywhere and just wanted to eat some grass. It was important to get her to eat. To do this I could put milk or Italian dressing on her food. Ensure had recently been prescribed to add to her milk.

Been Kitty was another kitty who was no longer young. She was a tri-colored, multi toed, short-haired female. She did not know that she was no longer a kitty and certainly didn't accept being an old cat.

Shirley Louise was rescued as a pregnant female cat. She is long-haired black with white markings on face and feet. Where she produced a litter of kitties, she received her alternate name of **Mama Cat**. She can be quite unpredictable. She will look so cute and give you the "come on". Once you fall for it and start to pet her, she can turn quickly into a "hard mama" and give a swat or a bite.

NoNo Baby was one of Shirley's kittens that the guardians decided to keep while finding homes for all the others. Baby is a short-haired black cat who is full of energy and mischief. I was given permission to help try to shake the devil out of her. While playful, she shows none of the surprising meanness of her mother.

Iggy and **Norman** were lookalike long-haired gray tiger males. They were part of Mama's litter and went together to a new home. Later the person was unable to keep them so they came back home to Mama. They had sweet personalities and were relegated to the back room to keep them together. Iggy tried to sneak into the kitchen and was sweet and playful. Norman had a urinary tract problem and was unable to control his urine so he needed to stay where it was not a problem. He was sweet too but tended to be depressed and withdrawn.

<u>**Cassie and Schnitzel**</u> lived with a family in the country near the village of Hannibal.

Cassie, a large female Golden Retriever mix, took her job of protecting her home and family seriously. She was allowed to roam freely outside during the day on her property which was surrounded by an electric fence. She had a good-sized hole dug under one corner of the house where she sought protection if the weather changed to nasty before anyone came to let her in. When I first met her I was wearing a T-shirt that I left in her bed so she would recognize my scent. Her favorite treat was a Chew-eez dog treat and she loved having her tummy brushed. **Schnitzel** was a female feline with short hair and gray tiger coat. Her food had to be placed under a low cabinet in the kitchen that Cassie couldn't get it and her litter box was in the basement.

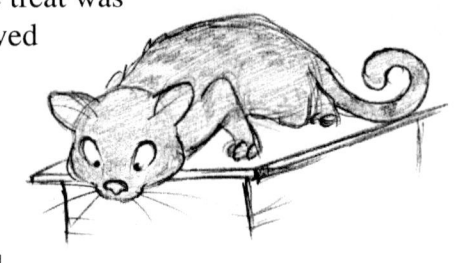

Roger and YouYou were two black Cocker Spaniels who lived with their guardians in the village of Minetto. Their house was away from the main highway, Route 48, which ran through the center of the village. Their house was a ranch style with a nice sized front yard without a fence that sloped downhill toward the street. There was a smaller back yard where a rabbit lived under the porch. These dogs were trained to go out without leashes and stay in their own yard.

Roger was an older male who was both blind and deaf so he had to learn to recognize me by my scent and energy. Roger was large and sturdy and intelligent. He constantly amazed me with his ability to adapt to his disabilities and his intelligence to know exactly where he was and where his boundaries were. It was similar, I suppose, to working with Helen Keller who is one of my heroines.

YouYou was a smaller black female and the daughter of Roger. She had lived her early years with the father of her current guardian. When he died, YouYou came back to her birth home to live with her father. She was happy and playful and usually unperturbed about anything.

Spot and Junior shared a home with their guardian, a widower, in the city of Fulton on the east side of the river. They were indoor cats who owned their home. Their house had a closed in front porch which helped to secure their indoor status when they tried to slip out as I entered the house. They were both white short-haired cats with black spots or markings.

Spot was older and more sedate. He provided a calm atmosphere and played respectfully knowing that humans have thin skin. Spot had known and loved the wife of his guardian and still missed her.

Junior was still a young kitty who had been brought in to provide companionship for Spot. Junior had high energy, love of play and had no idea why people were upset when he put his claws out while playing. He was curious and totally unpredictable except that you knew he was always going to be "into something". He insisted on satisfying his curiosity!

Winter 2001 Tales from the Tattle-Tale

When the family returned, there had to be an accounting of activities at home during their absence. Most of the time, the record showed that the little dogs laughed and the little cats fiddled around without causing too much mischief. The dates indicate the last day of care and not necessarily the length of the time spent with the pets. It's used to indicate season which affected weather and outside activities and sometimes accessibility to the home. An effort was made not to play favorites. It was an attempt at honest reporting from my point of view.

Report Card: October 3

Moon:

Since Moon was in the house when I arrived for the first visit we had a chance to bond before I let him out. He lay in my lap for a while and let me pet him until we came to a good understanding of one another.

On Saturday, he came out of "the swamp" when I whistled. He was complaining about the interruption of his hunting but he came.

After that day, he came when he decided to come no matter how much I whistled. Sunday night, he didn't show up until I arrived for my last visit around 7:30 P.M. I didn't see him, but I heard him as I got out of the truck. He led the way to the door. Monday he showed up in the afternoon while I was sitting on the back step with Rosie.

Tuesday night he came in late again after dark. While petting him, I found several burrs in his fur that he let me pull out without a fuss. Wednesday he was there when I arrived in the late afternoon. I convinced him that it was good to be inside at night, especially since the nights were chilly and damp with lots of fog in the early mornings. Inside we played hide and seek behind the large furniture and played "attack paws" on the stairs. After food, play, petting and brushing, he would settle down and usually sleep on the chair in the dining area.

Rosie:

Rosie was a good girl and stayed close to home. I tried to keep her in when Moon took his morning hunts because it was cold and damp all week in the early hours. I managed to get her to wait a couple of days until the sun was out warming and drying the ground. But Monday, she was determined to go out and leaped out from the inside counter as soon as I opened the door. I went inside and closed the door. After doing a couple chores like opening the blinds and cleaning the litter boxes, I went out to check on her. She really "bitched" at me, came inside and continued to "bitch" all the way up the stairs. I told her, "I warned you that it was cold outside."

We finally made a truce. When Moon went out in the mornings, I let her out and stayed out with her to brush her a little. Then she was content to come back inside until my later visit.

On the weekends, I came around noon and again later in the afternoon. On the weekdays, I just came once in the afternoon (sometime between 3:30 and 5:00). The afternoons were all really nice and that's when Rosie would be out. I sat outside on the back steps and read or brushed her. Then we got out the wet food before I left.

Rosie was only outside while I was there. I made sure that she was inside before I left. Her eye seems to be light sensitive (as you pointed out). It got very runny only when she was in the sunlight. I wiped it each day as needed with a damp tissue.

House Notes: You made my job easy. I closed blinds at night. I opened them in the morning. I put the trash out and placed it with the mail on your table.

Your calls, informing me of your arrival in Denver and later in Atlanta, were appreciated and reassuring. I passed on your messages to "your kids" attempting to imitate your voice as I said to them: "Hey Moon! Hey Rosie! Their faces showed recognition!

Report Card: October 22

Emmy Lou:

Did you know that Emmy Lou is a thief?
I spent quite a bit of time sitting and reading
to provide human presence. Emmy would
often get up on my lap. One day as I got
into my story, I noticed that she slipped
off of my lap and sat down next to
Molly on the floor. After a while I
became aware of a chewing sound.
She had found the dog biscuits that I
always carry in my jacket pockets.
The jacket was hanging over
the back of a chair which
placed the pockets at the right
height for her to nose in and get
at the contents.
Other than that incident, she was a model of good behavior. She came when called. She sat for her treats. She went to her crate on command.

Molly Brown:

Molly was so good! I
was uneasy at first with
her being off leash
for fear she wouldn't
come when I called
her. She has such boundless
energy! The first morning after
their first trip outside where they
responded well to the command to
"get busy," I spent a long time inside

with them. I fed them, sat with them, brushed and petted them.
This gave them time to get used to me.
Later when we went outside for a longer walk, I put a leash on
Molly. She was good about not pulling away but staying close and
obeying my commands. After that I was more comfortable and
didn't use the leash again. The only exception was one morning
when I had trouble getting the back door open, so I used the leash
going out of the front door.
She was a very good girl and very patient with me. I gave her a lot
of time out in the kennel on Saturday and Sunday.

Flopsy:

Flopsy stayed quietly upstairs away from the
dogs. She would come downstairs for a little
petting after the dogs were in their crates.

Rocky:

Rocky was as good as ever. I
couldn't get over how much he had
grown. Do you think that I will be
feeding him in the bathtub when you go
back to Maine at Thanksgiving?

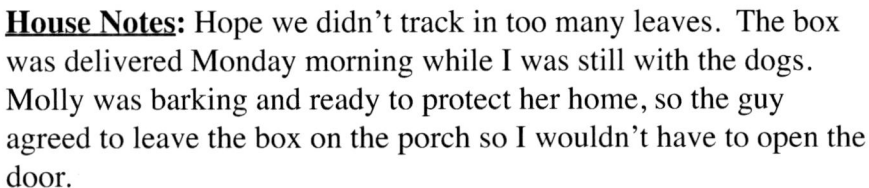

House Notes: Hope we didn't track in too many leaves. The box
was delivered Monday morning while I was still with the dogs.
Molly was barking and ready to protect her home, so the guy
agreed to leave the box on the porch so I wouldn't have to open the
door.

Abdual:

For the first three days, Abdual
was quietly invisible. I called
to her each day and talked to
her. One day I got down on
the floor and using the flash
light I verified that she still
existed.

Halloween came. In the morning, I got down on
the floor, lifted the ruffle and talked to her until I could see some
motion which was mostly just a head turn. That night while I was
cleaning the litter box in the next room, I talked to her as I worked
and took a little longer fussing with a spot. All of a sudden I realized that a calico cat was rubbing against my leg and it wasn't
Been Kitty.

After that, each morning and evening she came out from under the
bed IF I got down on the floor and talked her out. I told her that
her family would be so proud of her.

Downstairs:

Sebastian:

Sebastian is a dear old lady. She knows how to make the most of
her position. She seemed to be low on energy, but she could rise
to the occasion if Baby or Been Kitty got too pushy with her. We
spent time together on the couch and she always let me know when
she was ready for her milk. She seemed to know when everyone else was taken care of and had settled down. She would then
proceed to the kitchen table and wait for her milk. She lapped up
her milk laced with Ensure twice a day. She seemed to enjoy a
light touch or stroke, except one day she seemed
to moan each time I touched her. She was fine
by my next visit. She didn't seem to be
interested in going outside even though I
offered a couple of times.

Been Kitty:

Been Kitty took her seniority seriously. She hid from me the first morning. After that she was the first to "demand" the wet food in the morning and claimed my lap and petting space when I sat on the couch with Sebastian. She just couldn't get enough petting and rubbing.

She did respond to Sebastian, giving her space when she objected to being walked over. She would lie next to Sebastian and comfort her and keep her company.

Saturday night she put on quite a show chasing after one of the wadded paper balls. Both Baby and Mama just sat back and watched for a change.

Shirley Louise a.k.a Mama:

What a cutie! She lies in some of the most interesting positions. She really seemed to like to play with running water. She was frustrated by Baby when I threw the wadded paper balls. Baby just shot out first and batted them around. Mama was quite independent. She didn't mind my scratching behind her ears or between her shoulders but she did not take well to being picked up. She did get pushy when I was at the sink. Does she always help with the dishes?

Most of the time, Mama kept her distance. However, on the last night after Been Kitty gave her show and then fell asleep in my lap, Shirley Louise sat at my feet for a long time.

NoNo Baby:

I tried every day to shake the devil out of her. It just doesn't work. She is a good cat, though. She loves fun and has her nose in every-thing, but does not seem to have a mean streak at all. She was the easiest to handle and actually responded to my commands such as "NO!", "Leave Sebastian alone!", "Don't Bug Abdual now that she's come out!"

However, she would not stand back and let Mama or Been Kitty get the wadded paper balls. Sometimes I did see Mama or Been

Kitty play with them on their own but always keeping an eye out for Baby.

When I cleaned litter boxes, she always had to use it before I put the lid back on. Such a show off: standing with her paws on the side while she peed.

Back Room:

I felt like a teacher again. The first day, the kids always have to test your reactions. Well, the first day I found what looked like a regurgitated vole on the floor.

Concern: On Thursday I found a spot that looked like fresh blood on the floor. I checked over the cats the best I could, but didn't find any sign of injury. However, Akeem kept checking around the objects against one wall. I assumed that maybe an injured prey got away. But none of them would let me know what happened.

Harry:

Harry is such a special kitty. He just meets life as though it is wonderful. He doesn't know that he is having a hard time or that there are any problems. He responded well to brushing and petting. I'm glad you called so I could understand about the problem with his eyes. After that I cleaned his eyes each evening with the solution on a cotton ball. He didn't fight me but just seemed to think it was an interruption of his eating plans. He is an amazing kitty.

Akeem:

Akeem is absolutely adorable. She is such a square kitty. She is so sensuous and loved the brushing. She made little chirping sounds to demand more. Her coat is like velvet. She keeps her white so clean. She has such a bright look and that little black spot on her nose is like Elizabeth Taylor's beauty mark. What a show! She does like to sleep late in the mornings though. She usually wasn't visible for the first call but the wet food delivery always seemed to rouse her. As she got used to my routine, she began lying in wait on the couch.

Iggy:

Iggy is very personable but I think he's still angry. He makes a lot of demanding noise in the morning until that wet food is delivered. He gets everyone stirred up while waiting. He seemed to need a lot of attention. He rubbed against the kitchen door but then would run and hide when I went to pet him. Quite a character! And absolutely beautiful! Mama did a good job with her twin boys. The last few days, he used several opportunities to dash into the kitchen. He almost got himself stuck behind the stove. His back hips must have been wider than the rest of his body. Quite a sight as he tried to "pull through!"

Norman:

I tried to talk to him each day about the bright side of life. He may be depressed with his loss. "But look," I'd say, "you're in a place where you are loved." Sometimes, he actually looked less sad. He probably needs some grief therapy. While quiet and undemanding, he did seem to respond to touching and petting and my talking to him. These boys are really a sweet and good looking pair of kitties. After some time, Norman became friendlier and would rub his head against mine.

<u>Cassie</u>:

Cassie did a great job of looking after your home and property. She did seem to recognize and accept me on my arrival the first day and each time after that. She always came when I called her. But of course, she did come to realize that I always carried chew-eez with me.

In fact, Cassie came to regard me as a walking chew-eez vending machine. She has discovered that I carry the treat in a pouch at my waist and that's where her nose goes. Sunday night when I was trying to sit with them for a while, her addiction got the best of

her. The night before, she had been content to lie on the rug while I sat on the couch with Schnitzel on my lap with the promise that I would give her another treat when I was ready to leave. However, this time she lay as long as she could. Then she whined a little and finally came up to me, rested her chin on my lap, and looked up at me with those beautiful, pleading eyes. What else could I do? I emptied my pouch and left her chewing contentedly.

Schnitzel:

Schnitzel made herself scarce the first day. She stationed herself on the top shelf of the bookcase watching while I sat reading and Cassie lay on the rug. By Friday morning, she was waiting to greet me. Friday night she came up and took over my lap. From that point on, she knew exactly what I was there for: to feed her and give her a lap to sit on.

House Notes: It looked like your mother-in-law was probably in on Friday. The mail was already in and the dishes were put away. When I came on Saturday, I noticed tracks on the road from your driveway and then noticed that the boat was gone. I assumed that it was removed by someone you knew because Cassie did not seem upset when I came in.

Report Card: November 17

YouYou:

When I came for the morning visit, YouYou was sound asleep and you would think as deaf as Roger. I got all the way in without a peep from either of them. She was very responsive and eager to please. She went about her business and always came back for a dog biscuit. She reacted quickly and positively each time I called her.

Roger:

The first morning, Roger was a little startled but then followed YouYou into the yard. Did his duty and I was able to guide him in when He came back to the door.

However, when I arrived for the afternoon visit, he was "put off" by my scent. YouYou had already run ahead outside. Then, as I tried to guide him to the door to go out, he moved away from me and went in circles through the house. He finally laid down in a corner in the back room. He aggressively and stubbornly resisted any attempt to guide him. At the later night visit, he continued in this mode and would not move out.

I wrestled with this problem/challenge through the night. I thought I had met my "Waterloo" and would have to admit defeat. When I arrived Saturday morning, YouYou was asleep on the couch and Roger was still in the back bedroom on the floor. I slipped a lead over YouYou's head and led her back to Roger so that I could keep her close to him and in front of his nose. Finally, he got up and followed her out to the living room. I coaxed him with dog biscuits. YouYou made sure she kept getting some too. I could get him to the door and hand him a dog biscuit. He would grab it and go back inside. Finally, I sat down and read for a while until he regained his confidence. When he went to the door on his own, I let them both out and he made up for lost time with "potty duties". He came back in on his own following YouYou.

Hopefully, he is now more familiar enough with my scent that he has regained his orientation and confidence.

Report Card: November 23

Emmy Lou:

Emmy was as good as can be. She came when called. She walked beside me like we were in a show. She was always regular about "getting busy" first thing when we went outside.

She took possession of my lap every time I sat in the living room chair. I loved watching her run down the stairs after we fed Rocky. This little Cocker Spaniel really has a different way of carrying herself and does the steps like a dance. She was a joy to take care of.

Molly Brown:

Molly is amazing. She has so much energy and so much strength but responds so well to commands and to dog treats. I did find though that I had to give her a little more time to "get busy". She needed to run and expend some of her energy before she could concentrate on bodily functions. I also let them have time after eating their food to settle down for awhile. Then I let them out for one more "potty break" before I left.. Molly seemed to need that little extra time before she was really ready to do her "duty". She is a beautiful dog and you have trained her so well.

Rocky:

Rocky knew exactly what I was there for. He also seems to me to be more comfortable with his size. The last time he seemed a little awkward getting around the tank. But this time, he maneuvered around the tank easily. I have enjoyed getting to know a turtle personally.

Flopsy:

I'm sorry about the loss of your Flopsy. I'm glad you dealt with her in a very humane and loving way

In *Flopsy's memory, I am donating $10.00 to the "Paws Across the County" organization which helps those who can't afford to have their pets neutered.*

Report Card: November 25

YouYou:

YouYou definitely associated me with dog biscuits. She would come to me, sit so pretty, and look at me as if to say, "Well, where is it? Didn't I do good?"
And she had "done good". She had gone right out and had done her duty.
She always came when I called her. She responded when I asked her to help me get Roger to go out. And, yes, she did get a few extra dog biscuits for being so good and helpful.

Roger:

Roger seemed to be much more comfortable with me this time. He seemed to recognize me. He even spent a little time sitting next to me while I sat and read for a while. I discovered that I just needed to move a little more slowly with him so that he had time to think things out. He likes to move cautiously. There was one little accident that I found near the door. But he managed to hold most of it until he was outside. We really were both more comfortable with each other this weekend.
I certainly enjoyed your dogs and I think that they are beautiful Cocker Spaniels. Thanks for letting me get to know them.

Emmy Lou:
Emmy was good as usual.

Molly Brown:
Molly was as energetic as usual.
They both loved the extra dog biscuits.
I let them out twice and we took a
walk each time almost down to the
river. That gave them a good break.
And me, too!

Rocky:
We didn't hear a word from
Rocky.

House Notes: Your son was
no bother either. I enjoyed his company and
was happy to help provide transportation.

Moon:
For most of the time, Moon Boy was sleeping or just hanging out.
When I came in, he checked out who was there. Of course, when
I put out the wet food on Sunday he definitely showed up for his
share.
I sat on the floor with Rosie for a while. When I laid down on the
floor to playing with her, Moon immediately lay on the floor across
from me and stretched way out. I think he was trying to show that
he was longer than I was when he was fully stretched out.
He never seemed to be asking to go out except late Sunday night.

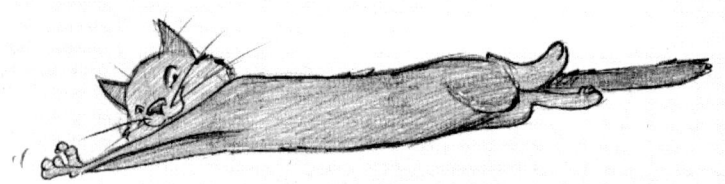

I told him it was too cold outside. He seemed satisfied and went back to sleep. When Rosie insisted on going out Monday around noon, then Moon came over and walked out the door. He was very careful to step in as little snow as possible. It was sunny by that time.

Rosie:

Rosie greeted me when I came in Sunday afternoon. She sounded like she was upset that I hadn't come sooner. She led me to the kitchen where I got the idea that she was ready to eat. She seemed to want my lap most of the time that I spent with her. She was sweet and friendly after eating.

However, when she went out on Monday and sat on the step just outside the door and wouldn't step down into the snow, she complained a lot when I picked her up and brought her in. She quieted down when I had her follow me to the side door down-stairs so she could go out where it was dry. By the time I went back in and upstairs to the kitchen she had come around the house and was waiting to come back in. I left her lying happily with her catnip mouse on her warm blanket.

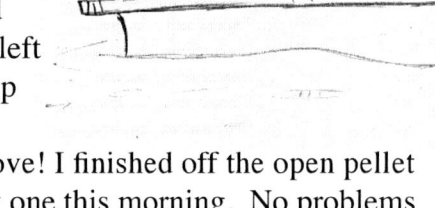

House Notes: That's a great stove! I finished off the open pellet bag last night and started a new one this morning. No problems with it.

Thank you for the early Christmas gift. I especially loved the picture of "your kids" on the card. It's a keeper!

Report Card: December 29

Spot:

Spot was really good. After a little reassurance from me that I was not taking your place and that I knew how much he missed one of his guardians who had died recently, Spot seemed to understand. At times he seemed a little withdrawn. He would play some until

Junior came along and attacked him
to get the attention. So I eventually worked out a routine with the
toys of throwing one pretty far for
Junior to go after and then throw
one to Spot. He was good
at catching and holding
onto the toys.
He became more playful
and lively as time went
along. But he was still
the disciplinarian when Junior was
overcome by his hyperactivity. He was very patient when Junior
attacked him wanting to play. He responded well to praise and
petting. He often sat on the coffee table in front of the couch to be
near me. He was always on one of the tables which were on either
side of the front door to greet me when I came. He never tried to
get out onto the porch and often would come sit on my lap for a
while each day.

Junior:
Junior was the true baby in the house, full of energy and curiosity.
He loved chasing after the toys and catching them high in the air.
He is quite the jumper. He responded well when I insisted that he
was not to use claws or teeth and was not to
grab my pants leg with his claws out. He
would get quiet and think about it
and then run to play with something else. Santa was quite generous with my cats for Christmas and
they chose to share a couple of mice
and balls with your boys. Junior especially seemed to enjoy them though
Spot conceded to check out the mice.
Junior only got out on the porch
once. Because it was cold, he was
easily enticed back in. He usually greeted me with his high

pitched meow. I soon learned that he is just a soprano and not in trouble when he "lets out" his high pitched song. He loved the running water when I changed their water dish. Occasionally I found new items in the living room with his toys. He loves the scrubber from the sink and once even brought in a fork. I'm not sure how he carried it.

I only found their food dishes tipped and spilled twice. However, one day when he was trying to come up be-hind me on the couch, he managed to knock over the lamp and break the bulb. To be on the safe side, I unplugged the lamp and ran the vacuum to make sure all glass was picked up. He said he was sorry.

Junior is as sweet as he can be when he finally wears out and settles down in my lap or next to me on the couch. Although he is still young and has some maturing to do, he is a sweet cat and should be a wonderful companion.

You are lucky with your two boys. For Christmas, I did bring them a treat of real tuna.

They've been looking for more ever since!

House Notes: As mentioned above, the lamp by the couch is un-plugged and minus a bulb. Your phone was on the floor a couple of times when I came in so I'm not sure if you got your messages or not. I just picked the phone up and made sure it was on the hook.

The dish of cookies on the porch came from your next door neigh-bor. I left them there since I thought they would keep better on the cold porch. I certainly didn't think you would want the boys get-ting into the cookies!

Hope you had a good trip. Let me know when it's a good time for me to come over and return the key.

3. New Year: Cold and Windy Tails and Tales

Meet the New Tails

These are additional pets that I cared for. The previously introduced pets continued in my care as their families needed my services. My practice grew by word of mouth since I did no formal advertising of my services. This venture into the pet sitting business began to feel like an expanding family.

Molly and Merlin shared a home on Route 48 about a mile north of the city of Fulton. They were later joined by **Max and Maxine**. I referred to them as the House of Ms.

Molly was a pure bred Old English Sheepdog. She was an unsprayed female as her owner had plans to breed her in the future. She was very large with lots of long hair that covered her eyes and had the usual rolling gate of her breed. She had a happy personality and would do almost anything for a dog biscuit. Molly was crate trained. Her large crate was big enough for her to move about and be comfortable in. She was happy and secure in her crate when at home without supervision. Molly loved to sit with people for hours but had to be coaxed to get her exercise.

Merlin was a short-haired neutered male cat with a grey-black marbled coat. His food and water dish were kept in a room that Molly was trained not to enter even though the doors were open. His litter pan was kept in the bathroom across the hall. He was the greeter at the door. Since Merlin was named after a magician he tried his magic of disappearing or "dematerializing" especially when you wanted to find him.

Max and Maxine were parakeets who came to stay for the weekend when their guardian traveled with Molly and Merlin's guardian. Their cage was usually in the child's bedroom with the door closed so Merlin couldn't visit unsupervised.

Kofi lived with his guardians in a two story house on the west side of Fulton on Route 48. I entered the house through a closed-in porch at the side of the house. I then accessed Kofi through a door that opened onto a small entranceway that either led forward up a couple of steps into the kitchen or to the right down a stairway into the basement. The kitchen door was left open so Kofi could get to his litter pan which was kept in the basement.

Kofi was a large short-haired orange tiger cat who had originally been attached to a person who had worked in Ghana. This prior owner had named him Kofi which meant "male" in the prior owner's language. The current guardians took Kofi in when he had to find a new home and they kept his name. Kofi had a very round body and the roundest, largest eyes that I have ever seen on a cat.

Mandy was the only dog in a one story house with a basement on the ground floor and with a front porch that was reached by walking up six steps to get to the front door. The front living room was separated from the kitchen by a partial wall which does allow for a movable gate to be used to keep the dog from the living room when desired. **Mandy** was a Shetland Sheepdog (often referred to as a Sheltie). She was a spayed female with Collie mix which gave her the longer nose of the Collie. She had a fenced in area in the back yard where equipment was set up for her to practice for her agility class and trials. Outside of the fenced-in run was a large area for good long walks on lead.

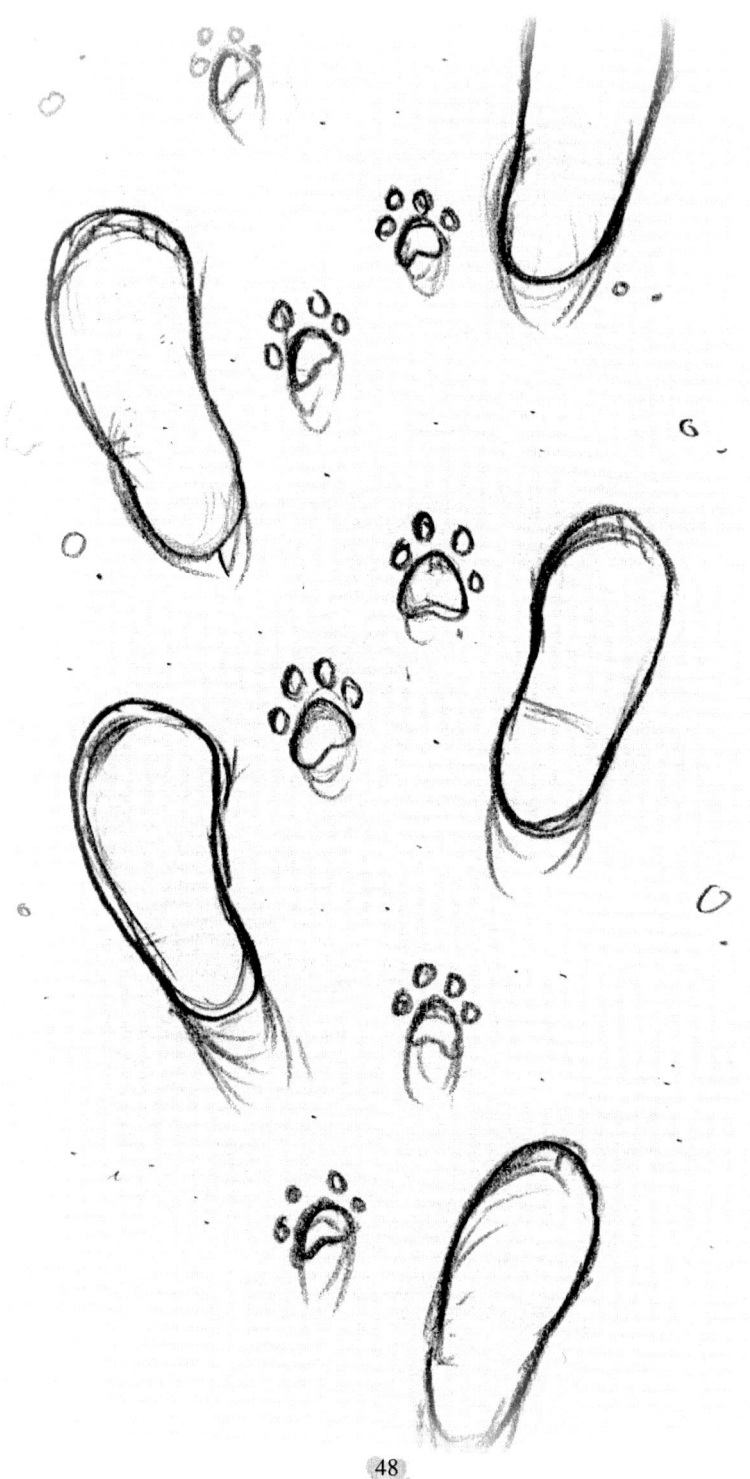

New Year: Cold and Windy Tales from the Tattle-Tale

The cold months of the early part of the year provide challenges in upstate New York for a pet-sitter who spends time on the road visiting clients. It provides entertainment for dogs who enjoy walking and playing in the snow.

Report Card: January 11

Molly:
Molly showed the sweet personality of her Old English Sheepdog heritage. She was just a gentle giant.
The first evening when I fastened her collar to the chain which extended from the line allowing her to run from the house all the way downhill to the river, she literally clung to the door. I couldn't encourage her to go further out into the yard to relieve herself. It didn't help that the weather was wet and gloomy.

However, the next morning, she went as far as she could on her chain. All the way down to the river! I walked down ahead of her and called her name. She would come running in her rolling gait so happy to come and get a hug. From that point on, she went out without coaxing to do her duty. We then had a good time playing on the hillside down to the river and back up again to the house.
She ate and drank moderately. She seemed to be happy just to sit or lie beside me while I read my book.

Merlin:
Merlin was as friendly as a cat can be. He came to greet me at the door each time. He wanted some petting and then would make sure that I checked his food dish. After that he left me in Molly's care and usually disappeared for the rest of the time that I was there. Occasionally, he would check on Molly and me. Sometimes he would

knock something off the counter or table to see if we noticed.

Sunday afternoon, he performed quite a show. Outside, the wind was blowing hard and tossing the dead leaves about. Inside, he was trying to catch the leaves through the sliding glass door. I teasingly said to him, "You might be Merlin, but even he couldn't work the magic of reaching through the glass." He is a beautiful and loving cat and took the teasing in stride.

House Notes: The only thing of note was the young man who came to check on my being there. Since I was unaware of his having watched your pets before, and having heard your concern about someone "casing your home," I called you about his visit. I hope I didn't upset you with the call but I felt better after your explanation of the situation. All of your directions were clear and I didn't have trouble finding whatever was needed for your pets. Hope you had a good trip.

Report Card: January 11

YouYou:

YouYou looked lovely with her hair cut. Her recognition of me seemed to be immediate this time and she responded well to my directions. She knew just how to beg for more dog biscuits.

I had no problem getting the drops in her ears. She was very patient with me.

A couple times when we went outside, she headed immediately for the yard of the neighbor next door (the one with all the lights at Christmas). Either she is using their yard to leave her "poop" or there is something very interesting over there. She came back when I called. Sometimes she just had to check out one more smell before coming home.

Roger:

Roger surprised me this time. Each time I came, I just held my hand to his nose before we tried to do anything. He showed immediate recognition of my scent and was then more willingness to take directions. I still held YouYou back so he could follow her on the first trip outside. Sometimes, the smell of a "meaty bone" provided the last enticement needed to draw him outside.

I usually stayed with them for a little while just sitting and reading. They seemed to eat better with some human presence nearby. Roger spent a lot of time checking me out, particularly the smells on my coat. He looked so handsome, and seems to be very proud of his new hair cut. Your groomer did a good job on both of them.

Note: I did find one mishap. "Someone" did his/her duty by the window in the room where we go outside. I observed that they ate and drank after we went outside. I started letting them outside a second time right before I left. I found that YouYou usually urinated again and Roger did his best "download" at that time.

Hope you had a good trip.

Report Card: January 13

Moon:

On Sunday, I went over around 12:15 looking for Moon. I whistled and called. No Moon! Snow flurries came and went. So I did some shopping and came back at 1:30. The wind had picked up and snow was blowing. Guess who was looking for me? Moon was very happy to come inside, eat some food, and sack out for the rest of the day. Monday was clear but cold. Moon was anxious to go outside but I made him wait until around 10:00. He picked up his feet carefully because the blacktop was very cold. However, he would not turn back. I gave him until 1:30 and then whistled and called for him. Before long, he came walking out of the weeds headed for home. After eating, he asked to go back out but I resisted. He wasn't too happy with me but I felt better knowing that he was warm. I have to admit that he is a good guy! Even when he is not pleased, he doesn't get mean.

Rosie:
Rosie was happy to just hang out didn't push to go outside, On Monday afternoon, after eating her wet food she up-chucked a huge hairball. She started this in the kitchen and she finished it on the rug in the living room. I think I got it all up without leaving a stain. She must have felt better after getting this out because she then decided that she wanted to go out," NOW!" I was the bad guy and said, "NO!" She grudgingly accepted and proceeded to settle down in her "Florida home" on the lounge near the pellet stove in the basement.

House Notes: Nothing of note to report. The pellet stove is great. Thanks for leaving the partial bags so they weren't so heavy to lift. I did open another bag the last time I filled up the stove.

Report Card: January 28

Kofi:
Kofi was a delight to care for. He greeted me with good manners and responded well to attention. He was quite interested in all the smells of my animals that came with me. He spent quite a bit of time checking out my boots, slacks and jacket. He probably separated out all of the smells for each of my cats. He looked like he was going about it scientifically as well as curiously. He did try to convince me that he was supposed to go out by standing at the back door and looking at me with a look that said, "Well, open the door!"

However, after two unsuccessful tries at this, he gave up.

Kofi supervised my filling his food dish and cleaning up his litter. He reminded me to freshen his water dish in the kitchen. We played a little game with his catnip toy. He seemed to like to catch it and roll a little with it. Then, when I would settle down with a book or the TV, he would come up and sit in my lap for awhile.

He was a very good cat. You would have been very proud of him.

House Notes: There is nothing to note about the house. I brought the mail in and left it on the kitchen table. Your neighbor didn't complain when I backed onto his drive to turn my truck around. Since Kofi used his litter box regularly, your trash can has received generous contributions.

Report Card: February 2

Molly:

Molly loved it when I told her how pretty she looked with her new hair cut. She recognized me right away. No problem going outside. We didn't have to use the towel after being outside but I did try to wipe around her mouth after she drank water. She was in the mood for fun. I hope you don't mind. For just a little while we some "gentle" tug of war with the towel. She was in a playful mood but also quieted right down when I told her to. Once again, she was easy to care for and went immediately to her kennel when instructed to do so.

Merlin:

Merlin greeted me when I first came in. When I filled his dish and went to say good-by after closing Molly in her kennel, he rolled over and begged to be petted.

At one visit, when I was sitting on the couch with Molly on the floor to the right of me, I ws petting her with one hand and Merlin came onto the couch and I started petting him with my other hand. Merlin, then, began to rub against Molly and reached out with his paws

to hug her. She just sat there, undisturbed by his closeness, and enjoyed the attention from both of us. I would love to have caught them on film with a camera. They were both so adorable together.

Both of your animals show all the signs of being loved and cared for and secure in that affection.

House Notes: Nothing to note at this time. Luckily the weather wasn't messy while I was there so we didn't track through the house. Thanks for leaving the cat food on the counter with Molly's food. You made my job very easy.

Molly:

Molly was very accommodating. Some of my times were a little off our regular routine because I had to work around a funeral of a dear friend. She had no accidents. A couple times, her need to urinate seemed a little more "urgent" but did not seem to create any problem for her.

I was pleased with her greeting when I came in. She remembered me and bounced around happily. She followed my direction to quiet down when I felt she was a little too rambunctious. We had some good walks down to the river and back. She was really very good.

There were just two times that I spoke a little more sternly with her. This was when she started to chase Merlin in the house. However, I think Merlin set her up and it was part of "their game".

Merlin:

Merlin was quite talk-ative this time. He frequently presented himself for petting. Several times, he sat

54

in my lap while keeping an eye on
Molly who insisted on sitting
right beside me. Occasionally,
he came quietly up behind
me and rubbed against
my hair. On arrival
and just before de-
parture, I searched
him out and he rolled over and talked exten-
sively.

I did notice when I was holding and petting him that he has a
"growth" (small lump) on the back of his head to the left side. If you
weren't aware of this, you may want to watch it to see if it grows or
get it checked out on the next trip to the vet.

House Notes: We did out best to clean our feet when coming in from
outside. Molly was cooperative most of the time in this process.

Report Card: March 2

Kofi:

Kofi greeted me each time I came. He would come to the door when
he heard the key in the lock and always spoke to me when I entered
the house.

He ate and used his litter box his litter box regularly. There didn't
seem to be any disruption in his normal processes. Each time that I
sat in the living room on the couch, he insisted on getting up in my
lap for a while. He was very accepting and friendly.

We played a little with his toys. He seemed to
like it best when I would threw
it right where he could catch the
toy. He came immediately whenever I picked up the brush which
I did a couple of times on each visit.
After each brushing, I gave him a
"fish" treat.

I brought some crewel embroidery
with me so that I could stay a little

longer with him. He was curious and checked things out but did not try to play with the yarn. (My cats would have torn me apart to get to the yarn.) He maintained his good manners at all times and showed gratitude for my company.

He certainly was a pleasant cat to be with.

House Notes: It snowed here Sunday night. I was surprised and pleased to find that your driveway was cleared when I arrived Monday morning.

I broke one of your plastic scoops when cleaning out the litter box. I replaced it with an extra one that I have.

Report Card: March 16

Routine for this day:

I was with Molly Brown and Emmy Lou (and Rocky) from 3:00 to 5:00 p.m. and again from 8:00 to 10:00 p.m.

In the afternoon, we took a walk almost down to the river when I first came over at 3:00. Around 4;00, I took Molly out alone with a toy and she had a really good workout chasing the toy. They both went out again around 5:00 p.m. before going back to their crates.

At 8:00 p.m., I let Molly and Emmy out to do "their business." Then, I fed them. They supervised my feeding of Rocky. I stayed with them for two hours, giving them plenty of time out of their crates while I sewed and watched TV.

Emmy Lou:

Emmy was sweet and very obedient. She stayed with me when we were outside following me very closely. She did "her business" almost on command. She was sweet as ever. She sat nice and looked expectantly when she thought she deserved a dog biscuit.

56

Molly Brown:

Molly played really well. I gave her a good workout, keeping Emmy inside so I could focus on Molly. She has so much energy, loves to play and to please. When I told her it was time to go in, she carried the toy in. I didn't have to pick up after her. She continued to hold onto the toy as she ran to the side of the house to do her "business". She never let go of her toy until I asked for it so I could put it away.

I worked with Molly a little. She sees me as a "dog treat dispenser" sometimes. She got a little insistent when she was ready for a treat and I wasn't ready yet to give her one. I held her off for a while so I could reward her for doing something good and not just because she knew I had treats in my pocket. She responded well to this little discipline. But then, you have trained your dogs very well.

Rocky:

I agree. Rocky has grown! He does look more comfortable though in his new tank. I was really glad to see the larger tank you got for him. He remains sweet and steadfast and responds well to attention especially when it is accompanied with food.

Report Card: March 23

Mandy:

Mandy barked when I was unlocking the door. Just what I would have expected from a good Shelty! When I opened the door and spoke to her, she immediately quit barking and greeted me warmly. She was ready to play but did not jump up on me. After I fastened her leash onto her collar, she sat and patiently waited. When we went outside, she was ready to run but then realized she had an "older woman" on the other end of the leash. She slowed a little and checked on me every so often. We took a nice walk everywhere that had been plowed. She seemed to enjoy the snow and became very playful. But no matter how playful she was, she still re-sponded well when I tried to re-direct her.

Inside she knew just exactly what was expected when I used the towel to wipe her off.

She offered one paw at a time and turned when it was time to do the back feet. She could not have easier to take care of.

Of course she got some dog biscuits for being such a good girl. We played awhile and sat together awhile. She certainly loved to be close and be petted and brushed. She was rewarded with a special treat of a couple carrots. When it was time for me to go, she again seemed to understand and accept and did not jump or bark. She displayed absolutely good manners.

Report Card: March 21

Spot:

Spot maintained his role as the "mature" cat with the quieter role. However, when I went to release them from your disciplinary "lock up"in the kitchen, I found them both on the top of the highest cup-boards.They came leaping and "flying" down while knocking a few items to the floor in the process.

After that first surprise, Spot greeted me quietly each day at the door. He would walk across my lap, let me hug him, roll over on the floor for attention and petting. But then he would go somewhere (in the kitchen, on top of a box, etc.) and lie quietly letting Junior grab the attention and my lap.

Junior:
Junior seemed to be matur-
ing. He was not as wildly
creative as he was at
Christmas. He is also
very intelligent: I only
had to remind him a couple
of times that he must not bite me. He remembered and
when I played with him he licked my hand instead of biting. He is
very sweet and craves affection. He would usually come around, sit
on my lap and ask for attention, let me pet or hug him and then dash
off for the next adventure. Monday morning while I sat on the couch
with the TV on, he ended up falling asleep with my arm around him.
He just seemed so dear and so trusting. Of course bribery might
have had something to do with it.
You really have two wonderful little boy kitties. They must be great
companions for you. I certainly enjoyed their antics and the way
they have developed in their play together.

By the way, I brought them a couple little mice toys that I had left
from Christmas: a green and a red one. I'm not sure where they hid
them so don't be surprised if they show up in some strange place. I
think Junior is the one that carries things around (like the dish cloth)
and leaves them in odd places like the middle of the living room
floor. What great entertainment!!

House Notes: Telephone: When I came on Saturday, the red note
from Alltel was hanging on the doorknob. I guess they were able to
fix the phone from outside. The problem must have been something
with their lines.

4. Tails and Tales: Spring 2002

Meet the New Tails

Springtime found more people traveling and needing someone to look in on their loved ones who had to stay home.

Jake and Sadie lived in the southwest section of Fulton. They reached their fenced-in backyard through sliding glass doors. This meant that I could just open the sliding doors and allow them to go out when they were ready. A family emergency was forcing their guardian to leave town for a couple weeks. Neighbor friends could check on her dogs and feed them in the mornings and most evenings. However, I was hired for just the midday visit and about 5 evenings when one neighbor was starting his vacation. Entrance into the house should be made through the garage so there would be no chance of the dogs getting out when entering the house. **Jake** was a male of Springer Spaniel mix heritage which accounted for his white and black coat. He seemed more relaxed and secure than Sadie. He had allergies and would need to be given pills if he showed signs of allergic reactions. He ate fast and would eat Sadie's food if she left it unfinished. He was playful but had a tendency because of a wide mouth to get a ball caught too far back in his mouth.

Sadie was a female, black Border Collie mix. She had been rescued from a bad situation and was slower to trust. She barked a lot when first meeting a new person, exhibiting fear and insecurity as well as protecting her home and guardian. If I could get her to accept a lead, I would probably have to walk Sadie separately from Jake.

Pepper and Sneaky also lived in southwest Fulton not far from Jake and Sadie. They had a great backyard but not fenced in so there were long leads at the back door where they could be hooked up and let out to run down the steps of the back porch into the yard. This was used at the beginning of each visit, especially important in the morning, so they could relieve themselves and check out the smells of any creatures that had wandered into their yard over night. Later, after feeding and some play in the living room, they were taken for walks separately.

Pepper was a midsize female black long-haired canine of mixed breed (Labrador and Terrier) who loved to run. She ran with her female guardian every morning which is what she missed most because I don't run. I just walk. I was warned not to pick up her poop right away because she was very aggressive in her attempt to cover it up. She kicked up anything loose on the ground behind her back feet. She enjoyed playing toss which we were allowed to do in the front room as demonstrated by the guardian. Pepper was very friendly and responsive.

Sneaky was a small male short-hair canine predominantly Toy Fox and Chihuahua mixed breed. He had been rescued from his street life and taken to the police station where one of the policemen fell in love with him. Since no one claimed him, he was taken home by the policeman where Pepper lived. They became great playmates. When Pepper would run after the toys Sneaky would run after Pepper. When Pepper got the toy, Sneaky got Pepper's tail and they ran hooked together like an engine and its caboose. Sneaky was less trusting (usually found each day hiding on a bed upstairs) and needed patience and coaxing to come down stairs. At least when we first met!

Holly lived in a mobile home. The mobile home park was about a mile north of Fulton on Route 48. The park ran along the Oswego River and provided lots of roads through the park for walking.

Holly was a small female Lhasa Apso who had been bred by the guardian and who kept her along with her mother until the mother died. She had a small body but a big personality and loved to take charge. When I met her, she had a chronic heart problem and had to be medicated every day. This was the first time I had the guardian be very clear about what she wanted if anything happened to Holly while she was in my care.

Pretty and Miasmo were felines sharing a home in Minetto. The house was a two story with a basement. A cat door had been created in the door to the basement where the litter box was kept. A decorative fountain in the living room area was their favorite source of water. They were allowed on the furniture and throughout the house. I was warned to not leave anything breakable on the table because they played chase across the dining room table. Also, I needed to be careful when entering and exiting the house, especially when watering the plants on the porch, since they did like to try to escape occasionally even though they were 'inside' cats.

Pretty was a black and white neutered male cat. He loved catnip and I was duly warned that he did bite. He was about one and a half years old, lively and friendly.

Miasmo was a black and white short-haired spayed female cat. She had more white on her face than Pretty. She was shyer and would take longer to accept a stranger.

Trixie often stayed at Mandy's home while their guardians shared business and vacation times together. She and Mandy were together a lot and were like family and best friends.

Trixie was a female, mixed short-haired breed with a predominance of Hound Dog. Her coloring was mostly brown and black. She had the nose and instincts of the hound along with intelligence, a sweetness that was endearing, and a strong will shown by her determination to sleep on the couch. The contrast of her personality with that of Mandy, the well-trained, mannerly Sheltie provided constant entertainment.

Chickadee and Yul lived in a small but comfortable one-story home a little west of Minetto. The house was surrounded by a yard with several small flower gardens and woods close by on two sides. Several windows had flower boxes. Part of the time was spent watering the flowers as needed.

Chickadee was a small female feline with a lovely long haired coat of black with precise markings of white around the face and feet. She was pretty and she knew it. She used her looks to entice you to pet her and would invite you in. Then, if you petted her one more stroke than she wanted you might feel her claw or her teeth. Her favorite spot was atop a small step ladder placed on a desk near a window where she could look out at the birds and squirrels and dream of hunting. She also liked the tall bar stool in the kitchen where she could supervise inside and also watch the wildlife outside.

Yul was a black Siamese Fighting Fish (Beta). He spent his time in a small clear bowl that contained a few water plants and shells where he tried to hide out. The cat left Yul alone but occasionally tasted the water in the open bowl.

Spring Tales from the Tattle-Tale

Spring meant longer walks in the sunshine except when April rain watered the new May flowers.

Mandy:

Mandy was as sweet and good as I remember her being the last time I was with her.

Of course, she did what a Sheltie was supposed to do and barked when she heard me coming. As soon as I was inside she greeted me playfully. For a Shetland Sheepdog, Mandy has a quiet disposition and really loves following directions.

On Friday, since the weather was so nice we took a very long walk all around the house and garden. She sat nicely when offered a treat. She enjoyed lying on the couch next to me for lots of petting and hugs and some brushing.

Since Saturday was a rainy day, we broke up the visit time with two short walks. She cooperated nicely when I wiped off her coat and feet. She knew she had been good so she insisted on her treat.

Sunday came and it was still wet outside but no longer raining. We took a long happy and "productive" walk. I wiped off the wet feet and she endured patiently.

House Notes: Thanks for leaving the towel out for me. We made good use of it and avoided tracking across your floors.

Jake:

Jake was friendly and full of life. He greeted me each day at the door and made me feel welcome. He loved the walks and was full of interest in everything and everyone. He was happy and fun-loving. When I walked the two dogs together, he would always fall back in step with Sadie after each distraction. (She may have communicated the message to him to quiet down and get back in line.) I loved the way he would literally throw himself on the couch next to me whenever I sat down on the couch to stay with them for a while. He soaked up affection and attention and enjoyed being petted and combed.

Jake would check on Sadie and follow her lead, but his friendliness and trust were helpful in drawing Sadie forward. His positive attitude was so pleasant. He definitely loved his treats and his food.

Sadie:

Sadie took her time accepting me. The first day she was very distrusting. To get her to take a treat, I would have to throw one for Jake to chase in the opposite direction and then throw one to her. Otherwise, she took so long checking it out that Jake would grab it first. She refused to accept one from my hand.

On the first day, after letting them out into the back fenced-in yard for exercise, I just lay down on the couch and dozed for two hours in front of the TV. Jake spent most of that time on the couch with me. It gave Sadie a chance to get used to me in a very non-threatening situation.

It took a couple of days to get her to finally take a treat from my hand. In a couple more days she got on the couch with Jake and me.

After about 5 days, she let me put her harness on her. Sadie, Jake and I had a nice walk in the neighborhood each day after that.

Sadie has such control and self-discipline that it was a surprise and pleasure when she came to me to be petted and rolled over on her back and exposed her stomach for petting.

Notes: I really enjoyed being with Jake and Sadie. I will truly miss them. By the way, they told me that the other friends who checked in on them were really great!
BUT they got most excited when I told them that you were on your way home.

Pepper:

Pepper has lots of PEP but is also a very good-natured and obedient dog. Each morning I reminded her that I do not run like her guardian and that her female guardian is much younger than I. She seemed to understand and we had some good long walks. When I needed a break I would ask her to sit. She always obeyed because she got a treat while I got a breather.

I think it is really nice the way she waits when I put them out back. I always put her out first and then Sneaky. Pepper would always wait to go down the stairs until Sneaky was out and seemed to be careful not to run too fast if their lines got tangled.

Pepper was very well tempered even though we did get a hot spell which sometimes affects the larger animals, especially if they have black coats. She was well mannered, greeting me at the door when I came and sitting when I tried to quiet her excitement. You can be very proud of her.

Sneaky:

Sneaky was absolutely delightful. He came down the first night because he really had "to go." He submitted to my "hitching him to his line," but when he came in he ran immediately upstairs to his hide-a-way room. I did what you suggested. I got down at the doorway in a play position. He jumped off of the bed at once and ran over to me and licked my face.

From that time forward he greeted me happily at the door with Pepper. I would take them out back. They got a treat when they came in. In the morning I would then take Pepper out for her long exercise walk. Sneaky hung around until we were gone and greeted us when we got back.

He played with Pepper while I watched. Occasionally I would get involved by tossing a toy. They would do their trick: Pepper gets the

toy and Sneaky gets Pepper's tail.

Every so often, he would turn and run up on the couch and lick my face. A number of times he really just snuggled up and wanted to be petted and held. He only snapped twice: in the very beginning over a treat and once when I went to get the toy he was guarding. When I reacted to this last snap, he immediately ran up and licked my face to apologize. I just can't imagine how anyone would have trouble with him. He was sweet and delightful.

House Notes: I hope I didn't mess up your lights. I forgot which ones were on a timer and which ones were not. I'll pay better attention next time.

Molly:

Molly was as sweet as ever. She is so patient and does very well in her crate. The weather was very nice most of the time. We stayed outside longer on the good days. We played a new game to get her to exercise more. I would get her to start back to the house while I stayed farther down the hill. Then I would call her and she would come running back to me down the hill. Besides the exercise, she loved the hugs which were her reward when she responded and ran to me. After a while, she started anticipating and turned back before I called her. She wanted her hug. She is just a large, lovable dog who thinks she's a teddy bear.

We also found some good late night movies on TV that we watched together past both of our bedtimes. She enjoyed the longer time out of her crate since many of the movies lasted about two hours. She spent a lot of that time just sitting with me. It did give her the opportunity to move around or sleep in a different position, like on my feet.

While Molly was very regular, it seemed to me that she ate less than the last time I was with her.

Merlin:

Merlin was much more visible during this visit. He usually met me at the door. Sometimes, he would be at/on Molly's crate. He really loves her. He likes to rub up against Molly.

One day, I thought he was dying because of the noises he made. I had closed the door to the bathroom to keep Molly away from the litter box. However, it was too closed and kept Merlin from the box also. Merlin let me know in no uncertain terms that he was very unhappy when he couldn't get into the bathroom. He also seemed to be getting most of his water from the dripping faucet in the tub. Many times his head was a little wet when I petted him.

He certainly was fascinated by the birds and was often camped out in front of the bedroom door where they were located. A couple of times he got a little pushy when I went in to check on the birds.

Merlin was more vocal during this visit. He ate more than the last time I was with him and he let me know when he was out of food. Could this be a sign of spring?

Twit and Tweet (a.k.a. Max and Maxine):

You didn't tell me the birds' names when you left the note about feeding them. So I addressed them each day as "Twit and Tweet" or "Chip and Chirp". When I entered the house each time I would whistle. Frequently I got a response from the birds. They were no trouble. I hope they're okay. It was smart to have the plastic on the floor around the cage. I forgot how far they can throw their seeds. Because of Merlin's interest and his ability to open doors that are not shut tight, I did add their door to my exit checklist at the end of each visit.

Report Card: May 2

Roger:

Roger seemed to expect me this time. He gave no resistance and followed a little direction from me. He went out each time without a problem. He did his duty and after coming back inside he ate and got a drink. Then, he would come to find me wherever I happened to be sitting and expected and responded to petting. However, he did not seem to like to be brushed by me.

You You:

You-You was delightful as usual. She did surprise me Wednesday afternoon. She was usually the one at the door when I arrived. However, this time Roger was waiting and You You was in a deep sleep. She didn't awake until I actually went over to her and placed my hand before her nose so she could get my scent. When awakened, she acted normal: She ran to the door. She went outside to relieve herself. Then, she looked for milk bones. I did break down and took a couple of milk bones from my truck for them.

One time when the sun was shining, she did her duty and while we were waiting for Roger to finish his tasks, she found a sunny spot and lay down on the blacktop driveway. She looked like she was posing to have her photo taken.

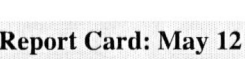

Report Card: May 12

Rocky:

Rocky was a very good turtle. He stayed in the tank even though he tried to stretch and with a little effort could probably begin to raise the cover of his tank.

He knew when I entered the room even before I started feeding him. He looked right at me. He seemed more agitated and hungry at the night feedings. In the morning he was calmer and more laid back.

Rocky is becoming a very beautiful and handsome turtle. The markings on his shell are lovely and I enjoyed watching how easily he moves and swims. It's been a pleasure and a surprise to see the change. By the way, is there an age at which he stops growing?

Holly:

The first couple of times that I came to check on Holly she barked at me. The first evening, she spent most of her time inside lying with her chin down on the floor facing the door.

After that introductory period, Holly never barked at me again. She was smart enough to know that I had come to take care of her. At each visit, we walked outside, she ate her food, took her pills and we played for a little while. She would then come up on the couch and sit in my lap. As you said, she put her paw out when she wanted more petting. She was always the one in charge. Then, she would get down and take a nap, usually lying on her side. I would pet her gently as I said good-by. She would look up and go back to sleep.

We had some rainy times. When I would dry Holly off after her walk in the rain, she would grab the towel and had a great time shaking it. That turned out to be her favorite game to play. Sometimes, we played 'shake the towel' even when it wasn't rainy outside. She would get a little demanding if I was too slow in providing her treats. We had a little talk about patience with slow pet sitters.

The last night I was with Holly she seemed a little restless unlike the other nights while I was there. I think she was anticipating your return or maybe it was the full moon. This time she was not lying down sleeping when I left. She was sitting up looking alert. Her breathing was good. She was not barking or distressed but definitely "waiting" for something to happen soon. She just knew that you would soon be walking through that door.

Holly is a happy dog. She has a great temperament. It is easy to see why you love her so much.

House Notes: A couple of packages were delivered. I placed them in your office.

Pretty:

Pretty Cat was always waiting at the door for me. He usually showed his appreciation for my services by eating something whenever I refilled their dishes and testing the litter box as soon as I had cleaned it out. He loved to check out anything I had with me like the notebook where I logged

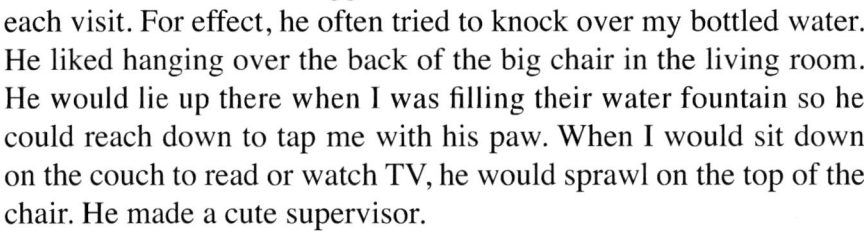

each visit. For effect, he often tried to knock over my bottled water. He liked hanging over the back of the big chair in the living room. He would lie up there when I was filling their water fountain so he could reach down to tap me with his paw. When I would sit down on the couch to read or watch TV, he would sprawl on the top of the chair. He made a cute supervisor.

Miasmo:

Miasmo would usually appear after Pretty had already welcomed me. However, as time passed, she began to wait at the door with Pretty. She loved to sit in my lap when I was on the couch and knead my stomach. Afterwards, she often rolled over on the couch so I would rub her tummy. One night I was watching a British dog show on the Animal Planet. She sat right in front of the TV watching intently. When I changed the channel she lost interest. However, as soon as I turned back to the show, she came right back to sit at attention in front of the TV.

As a Team:

As a team they were unbeatable. You were right that they tear through the house and over the table. I frequently had to straighten the tablecloth and settings. One day I found one of the napkins still in the ring by the front door. They wouldn't tell me who did it!

When Memorial Day came around, they ganged up on me and convinced me that since their "mother" was enjoying a vacation and special meals, they should get something different for the "Holiday". So, I shared some Tuna with them. They seemed very grateful, but of course they were disappointed when they expected some more on my next visit. They both enjoyed the catnip. Miasmo, though shy, became more aggressive than Pretty Cat when it came time for the treats.

I really enjoyed your kitties. They have such nice personalities, have fun together and responded well to attention and petting without becoming overly demanding.

House Notes: One day I found water in your basement at the foot of the stairs. Your son had been here washing his car and must have left the hose running at the side of the building. I couldn't figure out how to cut it off. I called and left a message for him and he came in a few days later to turn it off. We also had so much rain for a few days. With both of these incidents I found water in the basement. Of course, Pretty Cat had to check it out and in the process he got a wet tail and feet. The cats and I managed to dry it out or at least the area near their litter box.

On another day, I noticed some town workers repairing water lines. I later relieved pressure at all the faucets and ran the water until it was clean. Don't be surprised if you get a blast of air when you use the washer. I think all of your plants got watered. You are definitely taller than I am and some of them presented a challenge to reach and water.

Cassie:

Cassie just treated me like family. She was calm and cooperative. Friday evening, I didn't see her when I drove up, but when I got out of the truck, there she was right beside me.

Saturday morning, I was a little hesitant about going in because your sister's car was there. When I went in, there was Cassie coming down the steps with your sister. Your sister said Cassie spent the night with them. While we talked, Cassie came over for her treat and then headed for the door.

Saturday evening, I didn't see her around even when I got out of the truck. I went on into the house to check on Schnitzel. I must not have closed the door tight because Cassie pushed it open and walked right in.

I think she has the power to dematerialize and materialize on command!! I've known cats that do that, but she is the first dog I've met who does it.

She really enjoyed the brushing each evening, especially rolling over and asking me to brush her tummy. Satisfied, she would lie down and sleep for a while. When I was ready to leave each evening and gave her a last treat, she would head for the door. I told her,"No, Cassie,

75

you need to stay in now." She would just turn around and go back into the dining area and lay on the rug to chew her treat.

She was very good and made it easy for me to take care of her.

Schnitzel:

Schnitzel greeted me each time I came in and seemed to enjoy being petted. Schnitzel didn't seem to want to go outside. She was happy to stay in.

I tried to put food in her bowl first so she could eat if she wanted to while I brushed Cassie. I did slip her a little tuna. After all, you were all celebrating and Cassie had her treats, so it was only fair for Schnitzel to have a special treat also.

She is very sweet. She makes no demands and doesn't even seem to mind when Cassie eats her food.

House Notes: I brought your mail in. It's on the window seat.

Report Card: June 7

Mandy:

Wow! Mandy looked so beautiful running in the new pen you set up for her. She and Trixie had a great time together. Mandy led the chase and had such a good time dodging and twisting and turning. If Trixie decided to do something else, she teased her until she would chase her again and away they would fly.

The next day when she was alone, she didn't have as much fun

because I was too old to run with her. However, I did get her to respond to my requests to come. I usually got on the other side of the tire or the hurdle and she leaped through the tire or over the hurdle to earn a little treat. I can just imagine her responding well in a competition and loving the crowd's approval.

She is definitely a princess and knows that she is beautiful. She was very good. I see her maturing and responding better all the time to appropriate commands. You must be very proud of her and you have a right to your pride. You're doing a good job with her.

Trixie:

Trixie was very good and was a good companion for Mandy. She has a less hyper personality which helps to balance their relationship. It was good that they could be together at Mandy's home.

Trixie barked and jumped up at the beginning but responded well to any attempt to recall and use her training. She has a sweet disposition and does not demand a lot of attention. She did like getting a treat when responding to a command. Having the competition from Mandy for the treats really helped. Trixie, being a little hound mix, was not much interested in agility and jumping through tires or over hurdles. She was smart enough to see that if Mandy did something and got a treat, then she expected the same thing if she responded. Practicality ruled her motives.

She had a great time, particularly in the pen, with Mandy. They both

enjoyed the companionship, as well as the competition, and loved the chases. I enjoyed having the two of them together.

Upstairs:

Abdual:

Abdual was delightful. It was so nice that she recognized me. The first couple days she came out from under the bed when I called her name. The last day and a half, she was standing at the top of the stairs waiting for me. She wanted to be petted and talked to. She was very calm and sweet.

Downstairs:

Been Kitty:

Been Kitty greeted me at the door each time I came. She tried to demand wet food at every visit. I reminded her each day that we had wet food only once a day. When I took time to sit down on the couch, she was the one who insisted on walking through my lap a dozen times and then settling down on the arm of the couch. She really enjoyed playing with the wadded paper 'mice'.

Shirley Louise a.k.a. Mama:

Shirley Louise seemed rather subdued during these days. She hung back but kept her eye on everything. She did like to go upstairs when I went up to visit Abdual but her purpose seemed to be more in the line of harassment than just curiosity.
I gave her wet food separately so that she got some, but later I would find that she let NoNo Baby push in and fin-

ish it off for her. The same thing happened with the 'paper mice'. She looked like she wanted to play but then always stepped back for NoNo Baby.

NoNo Baby:

NoNo Baby was right there at the door with Been Kitty each time I came. She was usually on the stool. The last evening, though, Shirley Louise did take over the stool as part of the greeting committee and NoNo was relegated to the floor with Been Kitty.

She is such a beautiful black cat. Her coat really shines. She watches everything that goes on. Each evening, she insisted with those eyes that I steal a page from your notebook near the couch. I limited your ability to write notes by all the pages we used to play with. I did throw a lot of wadded paper mice for her to chase.

Back Room:

Harry:

Harry is amazing. He stays so sweet and loving. He responds to attention and brightens right up. His eyes do look better. I continued to clean his eyes each day though it seemed to bother him. But there was no meanness when he resisted the wet cloth on his eyes. I tried to tell Norman to learn from Harry and stop feeling sorry for himself. Harry didn't leave his previous owner to come directly to a nice home like Norman and his brother, Iggy. Harry was hit by a car and left on the road in the snow. His ears and his tail were frozen when he was found. His back legs are crippled. But Harry always smiles and responds well to attention and brushing.

Akeem:

I really enjoyed Akeem. She has such pretty defined markings. She looks like such a little toughie but she loves to be brushed and petted and responds with a great purr. She has a greeting voice that is definitely hers and very different from any other cat that I know. I enjoy her like some people enjoy little bulldogs. Each day I reinforced with her that her job was to keep out all mice. She would immediately go behind the couch and start looking for them.

Iggy:

Iggy is definitely the most forward of all your cats. He is "Mister Personality" in many ways. He demanded attention as soon as I entered the house. He objected to my brushing him the first day so I called him "Mister Hissy." But the next day he just rolled over and wanted to play. He even came up to me and asked to be brushed. I guess he likes to be in command. He wanted me to do it his way and when he was ready. Does that sound like his mother, Shirley Louise?

Norman:

I tried giving Norman his pill with the shooter. No matter how far back I put it in his mouth, he managed to spit it out. So, I put some wet food with it and put it in with my fingers. Those are sharp teeth! But we had more success that way.

I tried to tell him that he is loved and that he should enjoy himself and not feel sorry for himself. At first he seemed calmer. But I got the feeling the next night that he was losing his calmness and getting pissed at me again. Oh well! He is a beautiful cat and his coat is lovely in spite of his sickness.

Report Card: June 24

Chickadee:

Chickadee spent most of her time in the bedroom window. She

would let me pick her up, hug her and pet her. Then, I would carry her to the kitchen where she would be so cute rolling over to be petted and played with. But first chance she got in a break of attention, she headed right back for the window. I think she was watching for you. This was a good idea to get her used to me with a shorter time. She will understand that when you leave you are not gone forever. You do return home and I leave.

Most of the time, she ate lightly not showing much interest in the food. However, Saturday night she ate a whole can of wet food. I found an empty dish Sunday morning.

Yul:
Yul actually came out on Sunday, both in the morning and in the evening. He came to the surface for food and seemed to want to show off a little. All other times, he was well hidden in the shell or mixed with the plant so I couldn't tell the difference between him and the plant.

House Notes: I think your sister stopped by on Saturday. There were signs of someone else having been there. Chickadee said she enjoyed her visit.

Your plants are beautiful. You've put in a lot of work.

I watered a little indoors if the soil was dry in any of the pots. I gave a good watering outside on Saturday. I watered less generously on Monday because it rained overnight. I tried to find the ones that would not be reached by the rain.

Report Card: June 29

Chickadee:
Chickadee is a very intelligent cat. She was pretty good but reticent in the beginning. On Saturday while she was sitting on my

lap, I felt her claws in my leg and thought that I might want to suggest that you have the vet cut her nails the next time she went in for a check- up. I'm not sure if that is what annoyed her or not but she reached over and bit my hand. I verbally admonished her and she understood that I was not pleased with her behavior. When I came back that evening, she was rather stand-offish and sitting on the little stepladder in the study keeping her back turned. I went in and picked her up and hugged her. Then I explained again that I was not pleased with her former behavior and that I did not take her guardian away and that you would be coming back in a few days.

From that point on, we have gotten on famously. Each day, she played more and insisted on coming and sitting in my lap. I used your afghan on my lap. It gave her something soft to knead into and apparently your scent on the blanket soothed her.

Most evenings, after some play, we sat together with her sleeping in my lap for a couple of hours while I either read or watched TV. Each day her recognition of me and her enthusiasm for play increased when I arrived. Then I started letting her know that you were coming home in two days. She seemed to understand, perked right up, and became even more playful. We had the best results in play with the string.

On the whole, she ate well. On the days when she didn't eat as much wet food, she ate more dry food.

Yul

Yul behaved well for a Siamese Fighting Fish. There were several times in the beginning that I was sure that he was dead. He did a really good job of playing "possum".

House Notes: Your sister was in on Sunday. I saw signs of her but did not see her. I put the trash out Sunday night. Found your recycling can upside down after the trash was picked up. It was then that I noticed that one wheel is missing from the recycling can. I saw signs that your person who cleans house was probably in on Thursday. Friday, I found the loaf of Montana Bread on your counter.

5. Tails and Tales: Summer 2002

Meet the New Tails

July and August were great vacation months for families so pet-sitting services were in higher demand for pets already visited many times as well as new pets who enjoyed staying home while the family vacationed.

Abby lived with her guardians in Southwest Fulton. The two-story house had a good-sized back yard that was fenced in and approached through a sliding glass door from the dining/kitchen area onto a porch and down a few steps. The yard contained several trees and a child's playhouse which were used in our games of hide-and-seek. **Abby** was a small female Border Collie mix with a long-haired black/grey/white coat which was always clean and groomed. She was clipped to a short coat by a groomer who described Abby as an aristocrat who cooperated but treated her (the groomer) like "hired help". She was always dressed with a scarf around her neck which accented her perky personality and smiling face. She preferred playing to petting and always responded well for treats.

Heidi lived on the west side of Fulton near the city line. Her home was one story with a large yard in back, a yard and large driveway in front, and a large field on one side. There was a raised pool in the backyard. When going to the backyard, we approached from the kitchen hallway out the back door and down a few steps from the small porch. If walking out front, particularly in winter time, we approached from the same hallway into the garage and out to the front walk and driveway.
Heidi was a female Beagle/Springer Spaniel mix rescued from the road. She followed her nose, which led both of us on our walks. She liked sniffing her way around the perimeter of the field border-

ing her yard and was always ready to take off after a bunny. Her guardians had first tried an electric fence but found that it didn't stop her from going after bunnies. It only kept her from coming back into the yard. She would sit on the other side of the fence and cry to come back in.

She had a cute little dog house in the back yard where she could be tied out during the days. She was brought in at night and was gated in the kitchen area. This is where she stayed during storms. Since she was afraid of storms, she was to be brought inside on rainy days. The floor was washable and the mop was handy in the close-by laundry room for the accidents that happened when she was frightened.

Missy and Hazel shared a dark brown ranch house in the country near Phoenix. There was an in-ground pool at the back of the house with a large area covered with concrete surrounding the pool. This area was enclosed by a high fence running from one corner of the back of the house around this area and up to the back corner on the other side of the house. The house and fenced area was further surrounded by a very large yard, particularly in the front of the house, providing lots of space to walk the dogs on their leads.

Missy was an older female Shih Tzu and Poodle mix (Shih-Poo). She was hard of hearing, aggressive with her food and not too happy with the intruder, Hazel. She stayed inside and was fed inside with a third of a can of wet food. She would be taken on short walks alone usually in the front lawn and then returned to her house.

Hazel was a one year old spayed female Golden Retriever with a lovely coat of reddish gold. She was energetic and hyperactive like most retrievers under two years old. She was kept in the fenced in area in back with a bungee cord on the gate since Hazel was able to open doors and gates. She was fed dry food outside on the patio area and there was sheltered space for rainy weather.

Chances, Moto and Cinder Cat shared a two story home at the north end of Baldwinsville. The upstairs was blocked off from animal entry. The downstairs rooms were all connected by open doorways, with a front music room with piano, another front room with TV, a living room with a couch, and a kitchen. There was a front door, but the dogs usually exited through the kitchen door into the garage and from there out to the front yard. The way the rooms led from one to the other gave you a circular feeling which was great for doggie chases. The front yard was large but not fenced in and could be easily accessed by people walking along the sidewalk. With the family, the dogs were allowed out without leads. However, I insisted that I would want them on leads.

There was a plastic pool that could be filled with the hose for the dogs to run through on hot days. There was a basement accessed through a door in the kitchen which was outfitted with a cat door small enough that neither dog could get through.

Chances was a 3 ½ year old spayed female Pitt Bull. She was the first pet the male guardian had ever had and he had spent a lot of time training her. She was probably the best trained dog I had ever met. On command of "No, Chances" she would immediately stop whatever she was doing like tugging on a toy or headed for an open door. Her favorite spot was lying on the couch that had been covered by a soft-fill comforter.

Moto was a one year old neutered male Boston Terrier. He had been added to the family who had researched to find the best companion for a Pitt Bull. Moto was high energy and playful. His favorite activity was trying to pull the comforter out from under Chances. His former training crate was still set up in the front room. I gained the family's permission to put him in the crate for a portion of each day to allow some quiet time for both dogs.

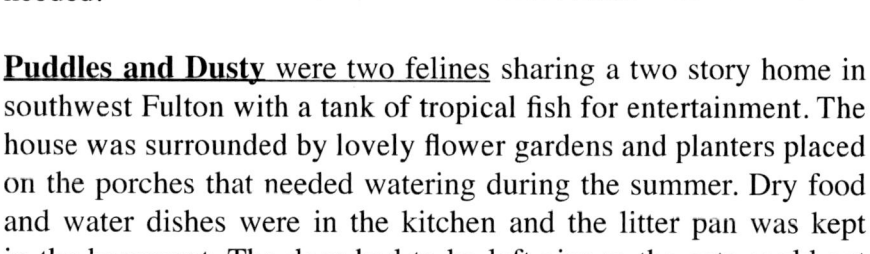

Cinder Cat was a short-haired charcoal grey female cat. She had living, sleeping and eating quarters in the basement. She remained in the background because of the highly active dogs. She could come up-stairs to sit in a window knowing that she had a quick exit when needed.

Puddles and Dusty were two felines sharing a two story home in southwest Fulton with a tank of tropical fish for entertainment. The house was surrounded by lovely flower gardens and planters placed on the porches that needed watering during the summer. Dry food and water dishes were in the kitchen and the litter pan was kept in the basement. The door had to be left ajar so the cats could get downstairs to it.

In the son's room was a planetarium type tank set up for **Lars, a resident Gecko.**

Puddles was a short-haired, black, neutered male cat with some white markings. He was handsome and knew it. He was arrogant. He was angry because he had to be an inside cat. I had to be careful not to let him slip out because the neighbors complained

about his venturing into their gardens. I always knew where he was when he moved because he literally marched like an angry soldier. He would come and stand at attention and give me orders. He was about 5 years old.

Dusty was a long-haired, grey, spayed female cat. She was older, about 12 years old, and a loner. Dusty was seldom seen since she was in hiding. If I found her hiding place and talked to her, she would find a new hideaway. She got her name Dusty because she literally looked like a grey dust mop and left dust and grey hairs behind near the food dish. That's the way I knew she had eaten.

Lars was a pet Gecko who had to be fed crickets which the son supplied in paper cups with a piece of carrot provided to keep them alive. He was camouflaged by the plants. I had to make sure he was away from the top when opening it to feed Lars. He was fast and could escape quickly. Water could be added through the screen covering the top or sprayed at him to get him away from the top. He preferred his light on during the day and off at night.

The **fish tank** was in the living room near large windows so it was not necessary to turn the light on.

They were fed once a day. They were no trouble but did provide a live TV screen for Puddles to watch.

Ace and Sarah lived south of Fulton near Phoenix, but still on the west side of Oswego River. The house had several levels. Entry was through the garage into a basement area where a large cage had been built by the guardian for Ace so that it accommodated his size. Sarah had a crate of her own. They both stayed in their special places when left alone at home. A very large back yard was fenced in and provided a great place for the dogs to run and play.

Ace was a neutered male Dalmatian about one and a half years old. He loved to snatch a treasure like a shoe and dash out into the yard as far as he could get from the house. He was a big tease.

Sarah was a small female Basset about one and a half years old and had not yet been spayed. She was the greeter with her Basset baying sounds. She was basically sweet and docile in personality and enjoyed lots of attention inside, but was ready to follow her nose all around the yard outside.

Marney and Bud were rescues who found a loving family in Minetto on the East side of Oswego River on Old Route 57. The two story house had a fenced-in yard.

Marney was a female Golden Retriever mixed breed. On good days it was okay to leave Marney outside during the day but never at night.

She preferred to be inside on hot or stormy days. She occasionally vomited but it was normal for her. She loved to play tug with a rope toy.

Bud was a white cat with some black markings. He had been treated for urinary tract problems and it was important to keep to his special diet. No treats! He stayed in the basement when no one was home because of his urinary dysfunction. I visited and played with him in the basement so we didn't take a chance on his getting outside or my not being able to get him back downstairs before I left.

There was also a son who might show up during the week.

Einstein, Beeker and Squeaky were an interesting trio who shared a home in Phoenix on the west side of the Oswego River. The home they shared with their loving family was a two story house with open access to the basement and a living room with a piano on a lower level of the first floor. There was a large yard surrounding the house with the house being set far back from the street.

Einstein, nicknamed **Einy**, was a large unneutered male Basset Hound. His area inside was the room with the piano. He liked piano music and was soothed by the sound. There was a gate at the entrance of his room at the top of the couple steps that led down to his space. His food alternated between dry and wet. He loved to be petted on his head and belly but I was warned to be careful of his ears since he often had yeast infections. He looked forward to his walks outside where he spent time checking everything out with his nose.

Beeker was a long-haired grey female cat. Her food and water were set out in the basement. She had a sensitive stomach so frequently

threw up in that area. If I couldn't find her, I checked under the beds upstairs where she deliberately went to avoid me. She was an inside cat but had full run of the house.

Squeaky was a "rich" hamster. I have read of hamsters that live inside a tin can in a small cage. Squeaky lived in a "recreation park." He was "caged" but had all kinds of tubes and rolling, moving crawl-through entrances and exits. Each tunnel led to food or water or bedding or to his exercise wheels. In spite of his generous living quarters I was warned that he was not friendly and was a biter. He was supplied with plenty of food. All I had to do was to refill his water and drop him a fresh cherry from the refrigerator.

There was a friend of the family who was also one of my clients who had permission to come and play with the pets.

Summer Tales from the Tattle-Tale

July and August means hot walks, pools, and finding ways to cool down. More blooming flowers need watering and those pools require some attention.

Report Card: July 4

Holly:

Holly was calm and restful most of the time while you were away. Because of the heat, I had to leave her in the bedroom several times so she would have the advantage of the air conditioner. She became anxious after she had an accident in the bedroom so I changed our scheduled visits. Since I lived close by and could just walk over, I came more frequently and even stopped in one night around midnight. That way she had less time between her walks to the outdoor latrine.

Often, it would have cooled down enough from the day's heat that I could leave her in the living room. She seemed more comfortable there. During the cooler times, when I left her in the living room, I left the ceiling fans on low. We used the floor fan with the door open while I was there. She loved lying in front of the fan.

Holly insisted on spending a little time on my lap during each visit. She drank a lot of water (we went outside frequently so she could pass it on to the earth) and ate well. She was so cute. Several times when she was just wandering around after her time on my lap, I would say, "Holly, it's about time you settled down." She would go over and lie down in front of the floor fan and go to sleep. She would look up when I left, but made no attempt to get up. She was too hot and tired to show me to the door.

She certainly is sweet and fun to take care of. I love the way she looks right into your eyes. I wish I could understand what she is saying. She certainly demands your attention with just a look.

93

House Notes: Mail and Sunday paper are on the table. In the bedroom, I used paper towels to soak up the little accident. I used the solution from under your sink lightly on the area to control any odor.

Abby:

When I entered the house, it seemed empty. However, when I called "Abby", she came down the stairs slowly (like a noble lady) and looked as if she had just been disturbed from her nap. All was said with a look with no barking required. We had to wait to go out until the young man finished mowing the back yard. When I went out with Abby, I played with her getting her to walk and run until she was able to have a good B.M. After running through the new mown lawn, I had grass all over my shoes, so I left them outside when we came back into the house. Abby refused to remove her shoes and was hesitant to let me brush off any grass from her.

While I was sitting in your chair to write my notes, Abby came up and leaned gently against me. I felt honored by her trust. She definitely wanted and enjoyed being petted. She even rolled over so I could rub her tummy.

NOTE: She found a dog biscuit that I had in my pocket. What could I do but give it to her. However, she did check it out very carefully before eating it.

Holly:

We were still working around the heat. Sometimes I left Holly in the bedroom with the air conditioner. Other times we were able to cool down enough with the ceiling fan in the living area.

She greeted me quietly Sunday morning. She took her medicine and then wanted lots of petting before settling down. The house was still cool. I came back at 10 AM to take her out again to relieve herself. Since Charlie was mowing the lawn where we usually walked, I let her lead the way down to the river. We spent a little time there in a shady area and she seemed to enjoy watching the geese on the river.

Later in the afternoon when I took her out for her break, she was favoring the left front leg. I examined the leg when we got back inside while we rested together on the floor. She did not indicate pain as I tested various areas of her leg and foot. I checked the claws and pads but did not discover anything. You may want to watch her for a couple of days to see if you think there's been a change that needs attention.

When I left her in the bedroom with the air conditioner, she didn't have any trouble getting up on the bed where she insisted on going. She may just have a muscle cramp from her sleeping position or developed some joint pain. But she definitely didn't want to be babied.

House Notes: Sunday paper is on the table. Charlie mowed your lawn Sunday – late morning. He wanted me to assure you that he would do it again next weekend.

Report Card: July 21

Heidi:

Heidi is a dear little Beagle with her sweet personality. But she is definitely focused on her nose when we walk. We took several long walks each day and her nose was to the ground all the time. She would not be distracted from her task of sorting out scents. She was very cute when the Springer Spaniel in her breed mix came out and she would stop following her nose and 'stand and point'.

She quickly got used to my voice and would roll over as I approached and let me rub her tummy. The first day I had to take her in early because of rain. She seemed a little timid and pensive and did not eat much of her food that night. However, she surprised me the second night and ate everything. Then, she met me at the door when I came for the late night visit and walk.

I stayed with her after the late night walk and read for a while. She would come and lie by my feet. I believe she slept well through the night because one morning I actually woke her up when I came in. She was still sleeping.

Heidi was a pleasure to take care of and a delight to know.

House Notes: I ran the pool filter each morning. Also, I did not have to clean up any messes unless I just didn't see them. It was good to have the mop handy.

Mandy:

Mandy is maturing beautifully. I loved watching her in the pen where she really loves to show off. She aimed to please as well as get treats for doing what she thinks you want. She took the hurdles so easily and flies through the tire. I loved when she jumped through and over them and quickly turned to come back through. It all looked so easy for her. I got a good workout just walking around the run and giving directions.

The first couple of days she was willing to try going in and out around the poles. She followed my lead well. Then, she decided she wanted to do it her own way. While she went in and out of the poles, she selected which ones to go around and mixed up the order. I think she tried to confuse me. She succeeded!

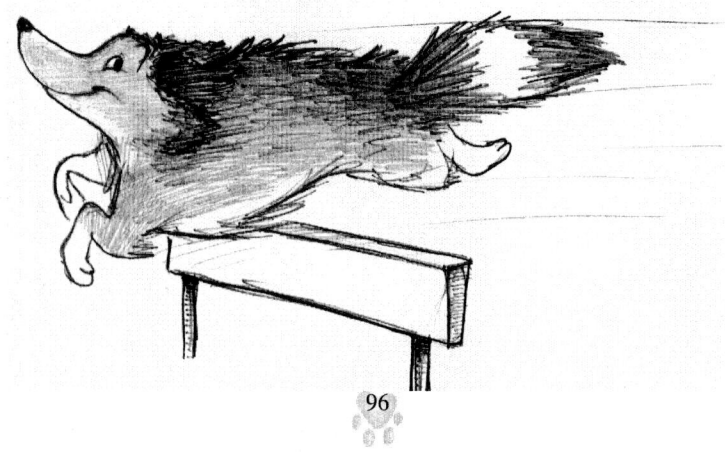

Trixie:

Trixie loved playing with Mandy and "staying over" at Mandy's home. They ran and chased each other all over the place in the pen. Sometimes, I felt out of control and had a hard time getting their attention. One day I brought a tin can with rocks in it. I shook it to get their attention. Trixie stopped immediately and sat at full attention. Though Mandy stopped, she shied away from the noise.

Trixie seemed indifferent to the hurdles in the run. Even though uninterested she did catch on quickly when a treat was associated with jumping the hurdle. Mandy helped with the demonstration. Mandy would approach running gracefully and leap through the tire or over the hurdle. Then, she would get a treat. Trixie would walk up to the tire and stand. I would hold a treat on the other side. She simply leaped through with very little effort and then wanted her treat.

I don't think Trixie particularly likes this agility stuff. She would rather 'track rabbits' or maybe even chase a fox.

Note: Mandy and Trixie would get so excited with their chasing and playing, that they would get exhausted and hot. After putting their leads back on them, I led them to a shady area where they stopped and lay down. I just stood and held the leads until they both were resting quietly. This helped them to calm down before getting a drink and treat. They also were less "rambunctious" during the remainder of my visit with them.

Mandy and Trixie are a great team. Their personalities are so different but they get along well and help to balance each other.

Molly:

Molly really got into our game outside: We would walk all the way down to the river. Then, after a while I'll say "Go, go" and she heads up the hill. Then, when I said "Molly Mop", she ran back to me. When she got to me, I usually gave her a little treat. She has learned to increase the number of treats by turning back on her own before I call to her.

She knows exactly what she's doing. I'm trying to give her more exercise: by running up and back down. She probably goes up the hill at least twice in this back and forth progress. She's managing to turn it into a "picnic".

She was good about going to her "crate" and so sweet in how she accepts and seems to like it. I did start giving her a little treat on my way out. So, a couple of nights when I was relaxing on the couch and trying to give them extra time but occasionally dozing off, she became impatient for her treat. She bumped me with her head, awaking me and then walked to her crate and waited expectantly for her treat with her head sticking out watching me with a big smile. What a feeling: Being told to go home by a dog!

Merlin:

I worked on Merlin trying to get him to eat more and begin to make up for his lost weight. When I filled his dish each day, I hid a couple of his treats in it. By the end of the week, he anticipated the treats but also ate most of his own dry food.

The first couple of days, Merlin couldn't be found when it was time for me to leave. After finally finding him in a closet I started closing the bedroom door when I knew he was in the living room. After that he spent most of the evening with Molly and me. He really loves her, rubbing against her back when she is sitting in front of me at the couch. So Molly gets petted by both of us.

At first he seemed a little tense but was his usual "congenial self" by the end of the week.

Max and Maxine:

Max and Maxine were very verbal singing to each other and also to me. Maxine spent time preening when I told her how pretty she was. Occasionally I had to ask Max to break it up when he was getting too amorous. On the whole, they seemed satisfied by their arrangement.

Report Card: July 28

Missy:

Missy was really cute. She didn't trust me at first. Each time I would go in to take her for a walk she would growl and hold back but she would let me hook the lead to her collar. She seemed to enjoy taking a walk on the lead. She peed each time we went out but I did not see her poop. She didn't eat much but I did finally get her to eat a little Saturday night.

Hazel:

Hazel is beautiful and a very smart creature. She was barking a lot the first time I arrived. After that time, all I had to do was call her name and she would stop barking. I tied her outside of the pool area with a fifty foot lead. Then I took Missy for her walk. Hazel would do her best to try to keep an eye on us. She just hates being left out of the action!!

She really did well except for leaving her poop on the pavement near the pool. No matter how long I left her outside the fence or walked or played ball with her, she seemed to save her poop for inside the fence.

She does know how to follow directions and will do anything to please. She is also very beautiful and will be a wonderful companion as she matures and settles down a little from her "high energy youth".

Report Card: July 28

Chances:

Congratulations! You have done a wonderful job of training Chances. She is very obedient. She is careful and caring with Moto. She is sweet and consistent. She enjoys her play with Moto but is really controlled. While they play rough, she is still restrained with her strength. She was very tolerant of me, allowing me to put her on the lead each time we went outside. When other dogs or people walked by, she responded to my commands to sit or stay and never pulled at the lead even when it got stuck on something. She would wait patiently for me to untangle or release it. I am really impressed.

Moto:

Moto, on the other hand, does not realize his lack of size and strength in comparison to Chances or to others dogs that pass by. He is ready to take anyone on! Chances is so patient with him as he runs around trying to get her to play with him and teasing her with a toy or trying to pull the comforter out from under her. He did respond though when I spoke sternly. He would sit right up and look at me with that wide eyed, innocent look. After the first day, when I left in the morning, he went right into the crate and settled down for the day. They both seemed to appreciate the quiet time this gave each of them with no need to keep up with each other.

Cinder:
Cinder or "Cindy" is really something else. She spent a lot of time first floor while I was there, on the table or in the window. During the times that the dogs were in the yard, she frequently sat at the door watching. (One day she almost got out when we were coming back in – but having failed the attempt, she didn't really try again.) When the dogs started playing their game of tug and tag, I would hear this other set of feet running for the door to the basement. She is really cute when she sticks her head out to see if the coast is clear before coming all the way through. I did brush her a few times. She really does have a thick coat. She seemed to appreciate the help with her cleaning process.

Group Notes:
The weather was hot and muggy several days. I ran water into their pool in the yard and they had fun cooling down. Moto loved to run splashing through it. Chances was more sedate.

One day I thought I had entered heaven when I came into the house. The whole downstairs floors were covered with "clouds" of stuffing from one of the quilted comforters. Somebody had a good time over night. There had been a full moon and the night was cool.

Another day while we were outside, and Chances and Moto were running around with their long leads I stepped over to the huge decorative rock in your front yard and leaned against it. Before long, Chances, tiring from play, got up on top of the rock and sat leaning against me. Moto was not to be left out. He tried to scramble up next to Chances but needed an assist. It was a crowded rock.

At one late night visit I was preceded into the driveway by 'kitty' with a wide white stripe down his back and tail. I put all the outside lights on before letting the dogs out since the skunk is a night creature and usually avoids light. The next day, the dogs got upset inside and were barking at a dog off lead that had come into the yard. We soon got a strong whiff of skunk odor. Your dogs didn't get the stray but it seemed like the skunk did.

Moto started pulling the second comforter from under Chances. The next day there was a re-occurrence of 'cloud cover' inside the house.

Moto was always ready to start something. He loved action and reaction. He would tease Chances trying to get her to chase him. Many times Chances would make the motion as if she would chase him. But she would then stand still and watch Moto dash off thinking he was leading the race. I could see Chances chuckling to herself.

Chances was very good natured and patient

with this active little terrier. She played the role of mother dog some-times by licking Moto and cleaning him. They are a well balanced pair. You made a good choice of mates!

J.E.B.

J.E.B. was a really good boy. He didn't bark when I came onto the porch. He recognized me and my dog biscuits. We had a nice walk each time. In the heat on the 29th we stayed in the yard or lower part of the field trail. In the morning, after things had cooled down by the rain, we had a nice walk all around the field. At home, we played toss with a couple of carrots and he caught them just fine. Each time we came back into the house, he went immediately for his crate and waited to be told he was a good boy and get "his cookie." We really didn't overdo it! Honest!! It may have been just the heat, but he seems to have settled down quite a bit in his more mature years. He took advantage of the opportunity to relieve himself when I took him out but he didn't seem exactly anxious to walk too far nor did he pull me along.

Derry:

Derry gets the **prize** for winning "Hide and go seek." He definitely outfoxed me each time. I tried to draw him out by telling him that his sister, Iggy who lives at my house, sent her love and wanted me to tell him hello. He re-fused to acknowledge the message and/or

the relationship and sent no response.
However, he had used his litter pan so I knew he was still there.

Puddles:

I called Puddles "Sergeant" most of the time this past week. He had such a way of marching through the house, questioning my presence, giving orders and generally letting everyone know that he was in charge. Each day, when I was out by the pool with the plants or skimmer, he would sit at the sliding glass door and demand, "MMEEEEE-OUT!" When I answered, "No!" he would turn and stomp off.

A couple of times he condescended to let me pet him and once he even let me give him a hug while he was eating his treats. However, when I would try to move him so I could close a window, he warned me that he had teeth and claws. This was probably just because I had told him, "No teeth and No claws!"

He is quite a handsome little fellow so I guess he has a reason to be very proud and demanding of respect for his authority.

Dusty:

Usually, in the morning, I would find a few grey hairs near the food in the kitchen, so I could tell that Dusty was still here. Most of the time, she stayed under the bed in the room with the window open. Puddles would be on the window sill most of the time. I would get down and look under the bed and talk to her. She changed from silence to a growl after 4 days. I tried putting a treat under the bed for her one day. She ate them while I was still looking.

However, I guess she regretted showing that piece of appreciation, so the next day she was under a different bed.

She really fits her description, looking just like a dust mop. I got to see her the night that

I put the trash out. When I went out to put the trash out by the street, I think she thought I was gone, so she slipped down to get some food. She was quite surprised when I came back in. It took just a few seconds of indecision, and then she was gone again. She definitely was easy to take care of.

Fish:
The fish ate and swam and did not complain at all. The last I looked at them today they were still alive. As long as I fed them, they seemed to be happy.

Plants:
Your plants are numerous and beautiful. The outside plants got watered every other day and the inside plants got watered lightly twice. Your fuchsia plant seemed damaged. There seems to be some new growth down by the ends in the soil so it might survive. The others all seem to be doing well.

Lars:
Lars was very good while you were away. But since it's the first time I've been this close to communicating with a Gecko, I'm not sure what is considered "good behavior." The crickets disappeared so I guess he ate them (though it looks like maybe one or two might have died and not been eaten). When I put the last set of crickets in on the 1st, the carrot had deteriorated enough that it slipped out of the line it was tied to. I was a little hesitant to reach in and get it.

Thanks for leaving your book behind so I could learn a little more about the Gecko. It's all very interesting. And it's fun now to recognize the green Gecko on the Geiko commercial.

NOTE TO LARS' BOY: In the American Indian culture, each animal has its own wisdom to share with us. The wisdom of the lizard (family that Gecko belongs to) includes Facing Fear and Controlling dreams. Lizard is the medicine of dreamers. He tells you to pay attention to your dreams. Dreams are very important.

Missy:

Missy seemed more comfortable with me this time. She came to me to put the lead on her collar. She enjoyed the individual attention. I had Hazel hooked up on the long lead, but Missy and I walked where Hazel couldn't get to Missy. She also ate better for me. She ate all of her wet food and enjoyed a few treats.

I did find the house very hot when I came in to get her, so I opened the kitchen and bathroom windows for some ventilation since they both faced the back where Hazel patrols the pool area.

Missy was a very good girl. Not even one growl this time!

Hazel:

Hazel, also, seemed to recognize me and was more comfortable with me. I was able to get her to settle down and relax a little more with me. Note: She did not have her chain collar on when I came Friday night. I looked around to see if I could find where she might have pulled it off. No Luck. So, I used an extra collar that I have with me so we didn't have to use the one that gives her shocks.

We played with the ball. She brought it back and put it at my feet and sat and waited for me to throw it again. All for a treat! It's amazing what she will do for a treat. She has a wonderful warm and playful personality. It was fun being with her.

House Notes: I like how you reinforced the fence! You have slowed her efforts to "tunnel out".

Pepper:
Pepper was very responsive. We had good walks each morning. She seemed to be okay with not running. She was easy to walk because she didn't pull off in all directions and kept a pretty focused movement until she had to find a spot to leave her mark. I definitely stayed out of the way of the "storm" she generated following her instinct to cover up her waste. However, (just like my dog) she did her digging and throwing too far away from her poop to cover it up.

She is very good-natured with Sneaky when they play. She initiated the play most of the time even bringing the ball to me to try to get me "into the game."
I'm not sure how good she will smell to you because she often found something in the backyard that she rolled and rubbed in. I'm not quite sure what set her off but I didn't see anything on her when she came in.
When they were finished playing in the front room, I would come back to the TV room to check out the weather. Since their food dishes are in that area, it seemed to generate more interest in their eating. Maybe TV means snacks to them.

Sneaky:
Sneaky was very loving with me this time. He always greeted me at the door and waited to be petted. Whenever I sat down, he got right

up and rubbed against me or came up behind me to lick my face. He seemed to have accepted me as okay. He was very good about waiting while I hooked Pepper up to the lead in the backyard and then got down submissively and waited at the door while I hooked up his lead.

Each morning, after I took Pepper for her long walk, I would take Sneaky out for a walk down the block and back. It seemed to help him feel equal and probably gave Pepper a break too, to cool down and relax.

Report Card: August 6

Molly Brown and Emmy Lou

The two girls were great, balancing each other's personalities. They definitely enjoyed the break Saturday, Sunday and Monday. Tuesday was a little cooler but still nice to be outside for a while.

Around noon each day, I took them for a run down to the river and back. Emmy was usually right at my heels, with Molly shooting off all around us burning up some of that endless energy. Molly never failed to respond when I called her even though it was hard for her to contain herself. The thought of a dog biscuit/cookie holds a lot of power!

They were very dear together in the Kennel after the run. When I came back for them around 3:00, they were so settled together that sometimes they didn't even hear me coming. We then took another run down to the river to use some more of Molly's energy and be sure they had a chance for one more "potty break" before going inside. They settled down so nicely in their crates. It was particularly very good on the three really hot days to be where they could get calm and cool.

Ace:

Ace was very good about going to his "crate." A dog biscuit would get him to go almost anywhere. He did enjoy grabbing something to take with him outside and tease me to come get it. You can see the items on the table that I retrieved: a teddy bear, one of your shoes and a glove. He even got one of my shoes and took it as far as he could in your big back yard. Then he lay down with it in front of his nose and looked at me with a big smile.

Ace ate pretty well, usually Sarah's food. He would come for a dog biscuit when it was time to come in. I had to catch his collar to keep him from dashing back out. However, once caught, he would go downstairs and into his "house." He settled right down especially if rewarded with a treat.

Sarah:

Sarah was very sweet, frequently rolling over to have her tummy rubbed. She didn't eat very much of her regular food at all, but was quite receptive to the dog biscuits.

She enjoyed running after Ace and getting him to play with her. She didn't want to go to her crate when it was time for me to go. She laid down, a dead weight. I would pick her up and take her to the top of the stairs and then she had to do the rest by herself. At that point she would run right downstairs and get in her crate.

Both of the dogs were very responsive. The first time I came, they barked a lot, especially Sarah with her little Basset baying. After that, they were usually quiet. If they started to make noise, I would speak to them before I even opened the door and they quieted as soon as they recognized my voice. They played together really well and were so dear when they lay together in the grass.

Marney:

Marney is a very sweet-tempered dog. She doesn't demand much attention. Most days I arrived between 7AM and 8 AM. Frequently, my arrival awakened her. She ate her food and was happy to go out and stay outside for the morning. I usually stopped back briefly around noon. We had several nice days that stayed cool and she was happy to be outside. However, the first few days and the last couple days were very hot, so she wanted in for the afternoon.

She ate well. Usually, at the noon stop and the late night stop I gave her a dog biscuit. She only threw up one time. It was when I gave in and allowed her a second dog biscuit. She enjoyed some light play. She was well-behaved and she looks so cute with the hair cut you gave her. It really helps her with the heat.

You've done a good job with your rescue. She is a real joy. You can be very proud of her.

Bud:

Bud seemed happy and healthy. He was at the top of the stairs to his basement home each time I opened the door. I fed him his three ¼ cups each day. His appetite never slacked. I refreshed his water each time I was there. He managed to clear two large hairballs during the week. He went a couple of days without using the litter pan. However, his appetite stayed good. So, I gave him the laxatone as you had noted. He really liked it! It seemed to help him with both his urine and his poop. He seemed to be doing well at the time that your son came and took over the care of the pets. In spite of his medical problems, he really seems to have a nice personality.

House Notes: Your son was at the house when I arrived at 6:30 P.M. on Friday. He said that he could take care of the pets through Sunday morning.

Mandy:

Mandy continues to get more beautiful and confident. She sails over the hurdles and through the tire with just a sign from me. Of course a treat waited for her when she performed well. You are doing a great job of training her.

She whimpered a few times when she went down the hall to your workroom and found that you weren't there. Then she came back and got on the couch with me to be consoled. Saturday afternoon, she even put me to sleep for a brief nap as she lay next to me and I petted her. We just relaxed and napped together. She was still on the couch when I "came to". She will be so happy and excited to be with you in your travels the next few days. I'm glad that you will be able to take her for the last part of your vacation.

I will miss Mandy but I'll continue to check your house and bring in the mail and paper. I'll rubber band the mail by days so you'll know when it came as well as know that I was there. I won't be leaving a report card on the mailman.

Molly:

Molly really looks so good when she runs down the hill. More and more she takes off and runs all the way down without stopping until she gets to the bottom of the hill. She is really a beautiful sheep dog and has such a sweet, playful personality.

Most of our days and visits were the same: take Molly out, go down the hill and play our game coming back. Treats for good behavior! Back inside, she eats and gets a good drink. Then we sit together. I tried to brush her each day as long as she would be patient with me. Just one time, she slipped back to the bathroom and checked out the kitty litter. I threatened to wash her mouth out with soap and she just smiled, but she didn't do it again.

Merlin:

Merlin sits and looks so wise some times. But I can't get him to tell me what he's thinking about. He has begun waiting by the back door when I take Molly outside. He expects to be picked up and given a good hug. He is quite a loving kitty, particularly with Molly. They have a really good relationship even though Molly likes to tease him now and then. I enjoy their interaction, especially when Merlin rubs up against Molly when she sits near the couch while I pet her.

Merlin ate very well. He is always looking for hidden treats that I put with his regular food to entice him to eat.

Max and Maxine:

Max and Maxine were very sedate. They did not put up much fuss. They seem to be happiest when the sun comes up in the morning. They were in the perfect room to get the morning sun. One morning I found the door open to their room. Someone took advantage of my oversight in not closing the door tightly enough. I wonder who that could have been? They didn't seem disturbed or upset.

House Notes: By the way, you must have worked a miracle in your bedroom!! Did Merlin, the magician, help you? I kept envisioning your room like a film being run backwards with everything flying back into its own place!

Pepper and Sneaky:

It is such a pleasure being greeted at the door by Pepper and Sneaky. They each have their own style. Pepper has learned how to jump up without jumping on a person. Sneaky turns "a million" little circles and given a chance will want to sneak a kiss.

I say, "Let's go potty!" and they run to the back door (but they do it several times back and forth and Sneaky adds his circles while I am walking it once). Then, they are so polite. They get in line. Pepper could easily push right out and run on but she waits patiently while I fumble with her lead and that "tough" clip at the end of the lead. It's effective but I fumble with it every time and she waits patiently. Meantime, Sneaky has been patiently waiting his turn. As Pepper goes on outside, he is so cute the way he gets down to the floor and waits for me to clip on his lead. Then, when he goes outside he sort of waits to see if I'm coming too. If I do, he gets excited and winds his lead around

113

my feet. So usually I send them on out and then may follow down afterwards.

Saturday morning, it was raining when I arrived. After they both had their chance to go to the back yard, I did walk Pepper in the rain (it wasn't a heavy rain, just a steady rain like we really needed.) We went the usual distance since it wasn't a heavy rain. When we got back I found that you had not left out a towel to dry them off. I took one of your towels from the downstairs bathroom because it was handy and I didn't want Pepper tracking on your new rug. (Sorry. The towel looked new but Pepper was so wet!) Because I was wet and a little chilled, I did not take Sneaky for a walk that morning. I had made sure that he got a good BM when he went out in the back yard.

I explained to him why I wasn't taking him out. I think he understood but was disappointed. In the afternoon, he held back a little on his affection (he hadn't really forgiven me or gotten over his disappointment). However, by nighttime, it was a "thing of the past." I promised to make up for it on Sunday morning.

I noted that in their play, Sneaky has added some new moves. One thing I had not seen before is the way he lies down on his back in front of Pepper while she has a ball or toy in her mouth and reaches up with his front paws "pretending" to try to take it from her.

Report Card: August 26

Einstein:
Einy did fine on the first day. We had a nice walk both times out – at night he was ready to run after a deer feeding on the apples. When your friend was here playing with your pets on Saturday, I began

to think they really partied Saturday night. When I came in on Sunday morning, he was so sound asleep that he didn't even hear me come in. And he had bags under his eyes! Starting Sunday night, he began "Hounding me" in the sense that he barked or "Bayed" a lot. I kept giving him dog biscuits because that's what I thought he wanted. But he couldn't be quieted, except a little when I played the piano. He seemed restless and I was beginning to feel a little irritated by his barking and disquiet. However, (and I don't think that this is just a coincidence) after you called on Friday to let me know that your father-in-law had gotten terribly sick on Sunday and was just now coming out of ICU, Einstein quieted right down. He didn't bark anymore, he slept more and he began to eat his own food again. He would come to the top step of his area to greet me and to say good-by, but he did not bark. He just looked at me very peacefully and was happy for a last pet on the head before I left.

One thing that I found that he really liked was for me to take a wet cloth and wipe his nose and forehead.

Beeker:

Beeker was a typical cat in that she liked to decide who she liked and who she didn't like. She is a sweetie and a beautiful little cat, but she took a while to warm up to me. I think it was partly because of your placing her in my arms as her introduction. You only know her as a loving and sweet kitty so you expected her to like an "animal person". However, SHE will decide who she likes. The best purr I heard from her was this morning when I got down next to her on the floor and explained that her family was coming home today. That's who she likes.

Squeaky:

Squeaky was very good and gave me no trouble at all. I didn't change his water since he only brought it down by a half of the container. I gave him an occasional cherry from your refrigerator. But Sunday, I decided he might like a change and brought him some grapes. He said he was grateful just by the way he sat there with one chewing away to show me he enjoyed it.

House Notes: You had a number of different deliveries from UPS (the driver thinks Einy is a good looking fellow). All of them are in the front hall or just inside the living room.

I usually turned the air conditioner on in the afternoon to cool the house down and clear the air. Then, as the cool night air moved in, I would turn it off when leaving after the night visit. Even with the fans on (and no air-conditioner on) the house would get stuffy so I took the liberty to open a few windows to help circulate fresh air.

Report Card: August 28

Holly:

Holly has taken the increased medication in stride. I think she is just happy to have the extra piece of turkey with her afternoon pill. She seems to be resting okay. The cooler weather helps a lot. I usually found her sleeping near the door. She didn't bark and took her time stretching and waking when I came in. Only one time did she seem to have real urgency to get out and she barked for me to open the door quickly when I arrived. I am not aware of her having any accidents and her bowel movements are good too.

In the late morning visits, Holly seemed to like going out on the porch for a while. After our walk around the yard and checking out food and pills and water, she always wanted a little time on my lap or next to me on the couch for some petting time.

Every once in a while she would get my attention and seem to want something. She has a way of looking at you without a sound that demands your attention. Sometimes she would want to go outside. I found that if I stayed long enough, especially during the visit after she had her pills, she needed to go a second time before I left. But when I knew we had just been outside and she was trying to get my attention, I would get a treat and we would play our game. I throw the dog biscuit. She runs to get it but doesn't eat it. Then I act like I'm going to take it away. She grabs it and takes it to a different spot and then eats it. I think she likes the teasing game as much as the treat itself.

Report Card: August 28

Molly:

Molly has made up a new game. When we play the game of her running up the hill and then come running back down to me for a hug and a piece of a dog biscuit, Molly bites the dog biscuit and leaves a piece on the ground. Sometimes, she deliberately throws a piece on the ground. Then, later in the day when we come out, she tries to find all the pieces she left behind. This is a good trick. It cuts back on what she's eating. It trains her memory to remember where the 'food is stored'. She also usually gets more exercise running around looking for the lost pieces. And we have a good time!

Molly did sneak back to the bathroom and got into the cat litter. We had a little talk about this. Some chastising language was used. I made a big scene of 'washing her mouth' and her face. No soap was used even though I threatened it.

Other than that one incident, we had a good and loving time. A lot of petting and brushing and hugging were the order of the day.

Merlin:

Merlin still looked forward to his hug when Molly and I came in from her run down the hill. I apologize for using up most of the cat treats. Merlin loved the game we played where I hid the treats in his food and he goes treasure hunting. In the process, he does eat all of his food. When I come in, he is usually near the front door. I think he is keeping Molly company while she is in her crate. They certainly have a great relationship.

Max and Maxine:

Max and Maxine seemed a little distressed by the fan in the bedroom so I turned it off. They settled right down and had what appeared to be a good time. They sang a little more and seemed content with their quarters. They especially like the East window where they can watch the sun rise.

6. Tails and Tales: Fall and Winter 2002

Meet the new Tails

Fall brings color to the landscape and some added color with new pets. Winter brings cold and snow and special holidays.

Boots lived in a two story house at the north end of Oswego. His litter pan was in the basement accessed by a door from the downstairs area. This door was to be left ajar for him. A downstairs room was set up with a lazy boy chair and a TV.

Boots was a short-haired, black and white neutered male cat who had adopted his current guardian. He was an inside/outside kitty but was to be kept inside while his guardian was away. He loved lounging with his guardian in the reclining chair and he allowed me to take her place while she was gone. He was four years old and very healthy and active. His food dish was divided in half to allow for dry and wet food and placed in the kitchen along with his water dish. He usually entered the house with his guardian from the back through the basement door. I was given a key to the front door where there were shelves open on both front and back containing some glass decorative items.

Gamin lived in Fulton on the east side of the Oswego River. He lived in an old two-story house with lots of rooms to roam about in and hide.

Gamin was a rescue from the streets of Fulton whose name in French means "homeless and neglected child left to roam the streets." He had a beautiful orange coat and carried the scars of a large male street cat that fought for his territory and food. His senior years were spent with his guardian and rescuer who even had the courage to give him a bath. He remained inside except for some supervised time in a fenced in back yard full of trees and interesting bird baths. He enjoyed the safety of his new life but also liked the feel of the earth under his large paws. He was doted over by his guardian who allowed me to watch him one time while she attended a wedding. What an honor!

Chewie lived next door to me on Route 48 about a mile north of Fulton. The rooms in the house were built in a circle so you had to go through one to get to the next. The kitchen was set up with a small crate, food and water dishes and newspaper on the floor for accidents. Folding gates were set up at both doors. Entrance was through the front door from a porch with about 5 steps up from the front yard. The driveway led down the side of the house and the front yard was small, placing the house close to the busy highway. **Chewie** was a small black-haired Yorkie-Poo about 6 months old. His short black baby hair stuck out all over giving him an electrified appearance. Electric would also describe his energy.

While unsupervised or home alone, he was gated in the kitchen. He went outside on a lead. His food and water were "served up" in bistro style containers. He was being paper trained to be able to potty inside. The paper needed to be picked up and refreshed.

Spike and Ella were two lively Yorkshire Terriers who shared a large older home in Oswego. The stairway to the upstairs had a banister with spokes that allowed them to sit on the stairs and see what was going on downstairs in the living room. The large couch in the living room was placed with its back to the large front window. It provided a lookout post for them so they could bark at all approaching bodies or even the ones that just walked by on the sidewalk. The dining room had a lovely well-lacquered wooden floor. A padded mat was placed at one end for them to relieve themselves indoors. I have never figured out how little dogs can have so much urine in their little bodies, which accounts for the fact that many of them cannot hold it for long periods of time. Vinegar water was always available to mop up the puddles that happened outside of the pad. Their food and water dishes were kept in the kitchen. A door in the kitchen led out back to a large porch with about seven steps that led down into the large backyard. Being in the city, it was fenced in completely. One side had a high cement block wall with steps up to it. The wire fencing was extended above this wall.

Spike was a male Yorkshire terrier. He was energetic and in charge. With each visit, he felt it his duty to patrol the yard and dash up to the top of the wall and march across it, master of all he surveyed. He took the lead in their 'house patrol' barking from the front window and then dashing to the side door where I entered their home.

Ella was a female Yorkshire terrier. She was a year younger than Spike and slightly smaller. She tended to be a little shyer than Spike and wasn't as compulsive about dashing outside, especially when the weather was rainy or cold. But inside, she was right with him protecting the interior from strangers and warmly welcoming family friends and pet sitters at the door.

Awin lived with his female guardian in a small two-story house in Fulton on the west side. The house was entered through the garage into a hallway with bedroom and kitchen to the left side and stairway and living room on the right side. The upstairs was gated to keep Awin downstairs and the kitchen was gated with him in the kitchen when left alone at home. A small fenced in area was provided in the back for off-lead play and could be entered from the garage by means of a 'doggie door'.

Awin was a neutered male Jack Russell Terrier. He had high energy and needed long walks at every visit. He was playful and inquisitive. It was best not to leave a pocketbook or bag of treats on the floor.

He was sure to find it and check things out when you were the least bit inattentive. His lead was hung in the garage. It was important to remember to close the door of the garage so that he could do his perimeter check of the inside before being hooked up to his lead for his walk.

Turbo and Bailey shared a large older home on a farm between Minetto and Oswego on Route 48. A group of **six 'barn cats'** shared an igloo on the back porch of this same home. The back porch ran along the back of the house and up part of one side to where a door led into the kitchen. There were about six or seven steps leading up to the porch from the side yard. A large semicircular driveway led from the house to outer buildings and entered and exited from Route 48. There was a large field that provided space for long walks in good weather.

A room off the kitchen, used also for laundry, provided ample space for two large crates for Turbo and Bailey. Their food dishes were in their crates and water was close by. In the kitchen, they each had a window with a bench for keeping an eye on the outside activities. There were several large rooms downstairs, but the one we used together most was the front room that had the TV and a fireplace (gas heater) with a carpeted space for lying about chewing on dog bones. The upstairs could be accessed by a front stairway or a back stairway at the kitchen. The full house was accessible for the dogs when they were left alone.

There was an employee who was a handy man who might be around outside. Occasionally a son might sleep overnight when on call for emergency service.

Turbo was a spayed female Golden Labrador mix. She was nine years old and required vitamins and 'Fit and Trim' dog food. She had grown up with the children and was favored by them when they visited their parents' home. She was playful still, good tempered, and easy to care for.

Bailey was a spayed female black Terrier mix. She was approximately six years old. She collected shoes, especially when the family was away, and piled them up on her bench in the kitchen. I was told that it was okay. Since she was a natural thief, had a black wispy beard and danced sideways, I called her "Fagan". She reminded me of the character by that name in the musical "Oliver."

The Barn Cats on the back porch seemed to be the young cats. The tougher and more mature fended for themselves and earned their keep by clearing mice from the outer buildings. These little ones had food and water provided on the porch. Their igloo was heated by a plate on the floor of the igloo covered by bedding and plugged into a socket on the back outside wall. The opening of the igloo faced toward the wall and left just room enough for the cats/kittens and not enough room for larger animals like raccoons. A bungee cord was placed over the lid of the can holding their dry food supply to keep these same raccoons out.

Fall and Winter Tales from the Tattle-Tale

Back to school for many but also time for weekends and even weeks for some in the colorful woods of the northeast provided work for the pet sitter. Labor Day, Columbus Day, Halloween, Thanksgiving Day and Christmas were times to celebrate with the Tails left at home for the holidays.

Report Card: September 1

Emmy Lou:

Emmy was very compliant. She stayed close when we were outside and came when called and was very regular. Each time we went out she would relieve herself. When she thought that she deserved a treat or just as a matter of habit, she would sit expectantly. She is beginning to show her age though so I took time to wipe her off when we had been in the wet morning grass and limited the distance of her walk a little in the afternoon heat.

Molly:

Molly still has more energy sometimes than I know what to do with. She always obeys though and comes when called and follows directions to kennel, crate and house.

Saturday afternoon I attempted to use up some of her energy before I brought Emmy out of the house. I think she enjoyed the focused attention on her. She started bringing me the ball so we worked our way down the hill and back up. She would run for the ball and bring it back for a treat. She ran and played so hard. When I saw that she was beginning to pant from the heat, I directed her to head for the house. She grabbed the ball and ran in tremendous zig-

125

zags across the yard as she went up the hill. She was a beautiful chocolate runner. However, I was concerned that she might have over-heated in the process. She went downstairs on her own and lay on the basement floor to cool down. I put water on her head and feet to help her cool down.

Today, she wanted to do the same thing but got totally distracted when a pear fell off of the tree.

Rocky:

Wow! Rocky is almost ready for the zoo, where he can be in a "tanker size" container with his own kind. I didn't see him on the rock at all during this visit. Is he able to get up there now with the size of his shell? He did let me know that he was ready to eat when I came near the tank. Good luck when you have to share your bath tub!!

Report Card: September 9

Boots:

Boots was exactly as you promised. He is very even-tempered and loving. It was a real pleasure spending time with him.

He never complained about his food nor was he demanding. He usually took at least a bite when I first put it down to show his gratitude. He used the litter box faithfully and is really "clean conscious". In his attempts to cover his waste, I would often find the plastic bag pulled totally over the litter.

He was very friendly. He always came to greet me and again to show me to the door when leaving. When I would sit in your recliner to sew or watch TV, he would sit close by and often come into my lap for some petting. But wow! What a pleasure and compliment when he curled up in my lap with his head nestled into the curve of my arm and went sound asleep. He was so trusting. It was very hard to have to wake him when I needed to leave. And then, he woke up gently and calmly and showed no agitation.

What a gift you have in the relationship of this cat! And I'm sure you are equally responsible in helping to develop and nurture his security and trust.

House Notes: There is nothing to note about the house. I brought the mail in and left it on the kitchen counter.

Chickcadee:

Chickadee was a little distant in the beginning. She tried to bite me at one time. I thought I had petted her in the wrong place but I think it was because she blamed me for "taking her mother away". Little by little she warmed up to me. After a while when she had been alone for a longer period of time, she really started looking for my company and play. It also started to cool down a little more. One day she surprised me by bouncing the little green ball and chasing it around the kitchen. I hadn't even seen it there.

In the beginning she stayed on the window sill in the bedroom. I would lift her, pet her and bring her into the kitchen where she would play a little then head back to the window sill. When I sat down in the living room, she would check on me once in a while but only came up to my lap a couple of times. After a week, she came in and settled down for an hour on my lap.

I usually checked her window sill when I picked her up in the bedroom. Saturday I found a large hairball. On Sunday I found the biggest hairball I have ever seen on her sill. It hurt looking at it. When she goes outside, she may eliminate hairballs by eating a little grass or greenery. But she had been in over a week and it had been very hot some days and she cleans herself constantly. Result: hairball – BIG!

While the bedroom window was her favorite camping ground, she

127

was found occasionally in the living room window – especially on some of the cooler days. However, the kitchen was her best area to show off in. She is so cute the way she balances with all four paws on the top of the cookie jar. One day, Chickadee actually ran out to greet me in the morning. In the evening, she made up for it by avoiding me totally. I started coming just a little later in the mornings. It was interesting how she would be "pacing" the floor, looking for me AND her food! I would usually spend a little time in the morning at the kitchen table making my notes or reading. It took a week, but she finally acted like a real cat by insisting on lying on top of whatever I was writing.

Report Card: September 17

Holly:

It is so delightful to see Holly with you. You look at each other with such love and acceptance and understanding. What a beautiful little companion she is!

One night Holly was unusually quiet. After we went outside to go "potty", she seemed to settle right down. I awoke around midnight, so I walked over to check on her. She really "binged" on dog treats. She kept coming back for more. She sat on my lap for awhile but seemed to find it hard to settle back down. I finally had to tell her to go lie down -- which she did. She was resting comfortably when I left.

Tuesday morning, she got extra turkey because she kept spitting out one pill. I wrapped it three times before she finally swallowed it. (I think she knew exactly what she was doing.) I didn't get a chance to toss her vitamin as you demonstrated. I showed it to her and was getting ready to toss it when she surprised me and took it right out of my hand. The rest of the morning time, all she wanted to do was to sit on my lap, so we had a good "petting time". I tried to do it as a gentle massage. She had a good elimination of waste so she seemed to be feeling good by the time I left. I had told her that "her mother would be home tonight." She kept looking for you. She reacted to every sound, checking to see if you were there yet. She is so smart!........and she loves you very much.

Report Card: September 17

Spot:
Spot was very quiet and restrained. However, he did not object to being picked up and hugged and petted. He still sits back and lets Junior have center stage while he sits on the table by the door. However, he does disappear once in a while to explore his surroundings.

Junior:
Junior is quite persistent with his high-pitched voice demanding attention. When I picked him up, he acted like he didn't want it. He kicked out and made loud verbal complaints. Then he would melt down and let me hold him tight. When I put him down, he would come back for more.

When we wanted to play, I didn't see any of their toys. So, I got the boys to help me search for their toys which we put in a box in the middle of the room. After we played each time, they had to put the toys back in the box. Guess how well they followed those instructions!

Report Card: September 29

Upstairs:
Abdual:
Abdual really surprised me. She must have heard my voice when I first came in and was talking to the cats downstairs. When I went up to check on her, she had come halfway down the stairs looking for me. She was

waiting for me each time I came, talked to me, and begged to be petted. I was so pleased!!

Been Kitty:

Been Kitty is really something for being the old lady of the bunch. She is so playful, talkative and was the easiest to pick up and hug which she seemed to like a lot. She also sat by the dish of cat food on the counter and demanded the wet food. She wanted it every time I came in. I only gave it to them in the morning. Have you changed the frequency of that routine? If you haven't, she wants you to! Been is also the only one who brings back the paper mice when we play.

Shirley Louise a.k.a. Mama:

Mama was rather standoffish (surprise?). However, when I opened the treats that were on the counter, she demanded them and gobbled up hers and a few others really fast. She then proceeded to throw them up. I reassured her that it was okay as I cleaned up her mess. Next time I came, I asked her if her stomach was feeling better. I think she appreciated the consideration because she really got into the paper mice game. I tried to clean up but I probably missed a few. We used up a whole little note tablet!

NoNo Baby:

She's still full of the devil but seems to be maturing and becoming a little quieter. She enjoys the paper mice but while she tries to catch them or get them first, she doesn't seem to bat them about like Mama and Been. She is a little less aggressive with the play and lets Mama and Been get a few more of the paper mice. She loves the wet food and isn't ready to wait for it when I'm opening the can, but isn't as verbally demanding as Been.

Back Room:
Harry:

I forgot to ask about Harry's eyes. They don't look as bad. Do you still clean them each day? I didn't see the solution for them. I did look at them each day and they didn't seem to be running. He is such a sweetie. I started picking him up when I brush him because he has to keep balancing himself when I brush him while he's standing on the floor.

Akeem:

With your change of furniture, where does Akeem go to find the mice? She is really cute with all the boys in the back room. Excuse me, but I think she just gives them the finger and goes on her own way. While Iggy growls at her, I believe that she would win any real battle they might get into. Her thick coat is beautiful and she is so sensuous, she really enjoys the brushing.

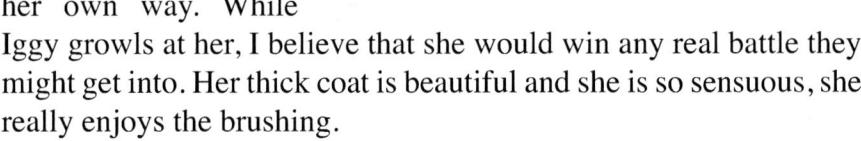

Iggy:

Iggy seemed full of "piss and vinegar" just looking for something to get into or someone to fight with. Most of it seemed to be just growling and threatening. He's like a politician, lots of promises and nothing to really show for it. I do enjoy the way he climbs on the fan on the screen door. He's always looking for some way to get the human's attention. I enjoyed his resourcefulness.

Norman:
Norman seemed quiet and really responded to brushing and seemed to like being held and petted. I'm glad he's finished with his medicine and I hope he stays well. I talked to him about trying to learn to "run for the box" when he feels he has to pee. He just smiled.

Note: I found one really large hairball in the back room – it was up where Norman and Iggy usually hang out – but I have no idea whose it was.

Sebastian is now waiting by the rainbow bridge for those who took such good care of her.

Report Card: September 29

Mandy and Trixie:
These two girls made a fabulous team. It was like having a "pajama party" and they seemed to have a good time. Friday was a little tough with the rain and trying to get them dried off. Sorry, but I grabbed the first towel I could find in the kitchen to try to get some of the water off of them, particularly off of their feet. It was quite a scene, holding onto their leashes so they wouldn't run all over your rugs and furniture, while trying to dry one and then the other. Needless to say, I got my face licked a lot.

They had a fun time in the pen in the afternoon

on Saturday and Sunday. The weather was perfect for outdoor play. In the house, they played quietly. As time passed and the newness wore off, they finally settled down. They became less competitive for attention and food. I found that they performed well together for treats. I would hold a treat in each hand, tell them to sit, and then lie down, and then sit up again with the treats right in front of their noses and then give them the treats. They were delightful to behold.

Each day, after getting them outside to eliminate waste and exercise, we would have "house inspection". I would turn on all the lights and walk through the house looking for "accidents". They got serious and followed me around, sometimes proud and sometimes anxious.

Note: Trixie only started showing signs of itching (and then not very much) on Sunday morning. I gave her one allergy pill.

Report Card: September 29

J.E.B.:
On Friday night, J.E.B. and I took the easy way out. Since it was raining, we took fairly short walks, just enough to give him the opportunity to pee and poop.

We were both glad to get out of the rain. I toweled him down which he was okay with but objected to my wiping his feet.

Saturday and Sunday were absolutely beautiful days, so we had long walks every time we went out. He was very good and we did not overdo on milk bones. At least J.E.B. and I don't think we did. The time he really anticipated one was at the top of the walk midway around the big circle in the field. We would stop. He got a milk bone. Then I ran the rake through his fur several times and we scattered our findings to the wind. He usually got another bone for standing still.

At the house, he would always go back into his crate. He would come out to get his food, his pill and a couple of carrots. When I stayed around reading or watching TV, he would come into the TV room and look at me to see why I was still there and not giving him his "leaving dog biscuits". I would tell him to be patient and he'd go back and lie down. He is so good.........and so easy.

Derry:

Derry came out of hiding! Well, sort of! He finally let me find him in the corner of the living room under the table with the lamp. I put my hand down so he could smell me. He wasn't ready for anything else yet. I tried, but he wasn't trusting enough yet to take cream cheese from my finger. At least he didn't run from me. When I was leaving Sunday after our noon walk, he poked his head around the corner of the living room door to watch me as I got ready to go.

I told him about his sister, Iggy who lives at my house, and promised some day to bring her to visit. My only problem is that she can hide as well, if not better than Derry, and I might not find her.

However, I think we made great progress this time!!

Report Card: September 29

Molly and Merlin:

I'm glad that you had the chance to meet my friend who looked after your pets this time. Since I transported her and came back for her after time in another home, I could guarantee that they had someone with them and that it was a good amount of time. It is very important to the quality of my service that the animals have an hour each time to help maintain the human presence in their lives.

Molly looks delightful with her new haircut. I stopped in a couple of times to help my friend close up. She has really fallen in love with Merlin so I had to make sure he didn't come home in her purse. That's a joke!

Kofi:

Kofi was so good. He seemed to remember me even though it had been a long time. He loves all the new things you've brought into his life: the wet food, the new bed, and catnip bag, and he really enjoyed following and watching the young man working on your ceilings, 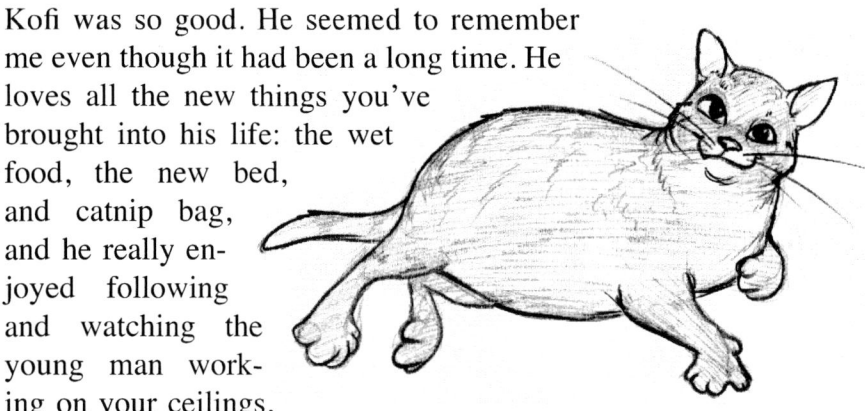 especially trying to hide out under his throw sheets.

Kofi was a very good boy. He greeted me, asked politely to be brushed and kept me good company while I was there even though the plasterer presented a distraction.

Kofi's personality seems to have gotten even "warmer" with time. He exhibits all the signs of being a much loved being and in return he shows his love for you.

House Notes: The plasterer was a very nice young man and a really hard worker. He deserves whatever you're paying him because he really knows how to focus on his work and be responsible.

Gamin:

Gamin was an absolute gentleman. He sang for his dinner. He asked politely to go outside. He walked about and checked the backyard thoroughly and then came back directly inside. He talked to me and thanked me for letting him go outside.

He then proceeded to follow me everywhere I went and gently, but persistently, reached out his paw to tap my pants leg as we walked about to make sure I paid attention to him.

He is definitely, even in his old age, a "kingly" cat and must have royal lineage. It was a pleasure to share his company.

Mandy and Trixie:

The girls are getting some of the routines down well. They're getting to know my commands before I give them.

When they see my two hands out closed – they know there are two treats and they immediately sit, then follow my hands as they lie down, sniffing to identify the treat, then come back to sit on command and take their treat.

I finally learned how to "save my neck" so to speak. When I take them outside, I get them to sit on the top step and "stay" until I walk to the bottom. They used to pull away and jeopardize my walk down the steps. They even stop now about the same time to pee – one on one side and the other on the other side. Several times they pooped "in concert". My problem is that sometimes when they finish, they're ready to tear off, usually in opposite directions. It's a little hard on the shoulder sockets.

I love to watch them sail around the pen together. What wonderful energy and

136

great exercise. To get Mandy to come, I call and hold up a treat and she's right there in front of me. Trixie gets distracted by a scent or a sound and does not respond very well when I call. However, she responds immediately if I whistle.

They were very good. Only one accident found – poop in the hall very late Friday night. I made sure that I visited them four times each day which seems to be better spacing to avoid accidents.

Report Card: October 9

Spot:

Spot was a lot more playful this time. Each visit, I would get them going with the toys. Spot became a little more aggressive in going after a toy, rather than sitting back and letting Junior have them all. He initiated some play, rough and tumble as boys do. He was very dear when I settled on the couch with the TV on. He came right up and lay next to me and for a short time on my lap.

Junior:

Junior looked forward to the play. He goes after the toys when I toss them but does not bring them back. I think he feels retrieving is for dogs. He was extremely loving. He likes to be picked up. He makes a noisy fuss and pretends to fight it off. However, if I put him down, he immediately comes back for more. Again, after play, when I settled on the couch, he cuddled up and wanted to be held and touched and petted. He actually seems to be growing up. He used his claws less and was able to settle for longer periods of time.

Junior enjoyed playing with the running water when we washed their food bowls. He was so cute with the water and of course got himself all wet.

Molly and Merlin:

It took a little while before Molly and Merlin stopped asking, "Where's your friend?" However, we soon settled down into the accepted routines.

Molly picked up the stuffy toy that sort of looks like a carrot and we had some playtime retrieving and tugging with the toy.

Merlin, after play time and love time, would disappear. I finally closed the bedroom doors so that I could find him when I left and make sure he was okay.

I'm not sure if it's the hair cut, but Molly seems to be more active. She was willing to go down the hill even when it was raining on Sunday. Usually she is ready to go right back in when it's wet.

Molly and Merlin have a wonderful relationship that is so interesting to observe. Merlin keeps Molly company while she is in her crate. Merlin started playing with the net that contained your son's balls. He was so cute. So I took a couple out for them. Molly actually retrieved for me. Merlin started out okay but got intimidated by Molly's size when she started running after Merlin's ball. He then retreated to the "safety" room. It's amazing how you have Molly trained so that she will not go into that room even though the door is always open.

Holly:

Even though the weather was rainy, Holly and I managed to time our walks when it wasn't raining or at least not more than a mist. We did spend some time wiping off her feet and making sure she was dry. That led to some good fun with the towel which she kept stealing from me each time I tried to refold it.

I had laid my jacket on the floor while drying her off. She managed to find a pocket with some dog treats in it and also managed to get her teeth around one or two.

Each time I visited her, she peed twice which is the heart medicine working. This afternoon she drank a lot of water and finished off her food. Then she came and insisted that we go outside.

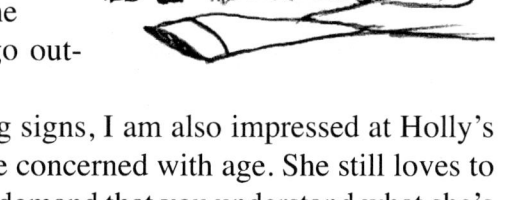

As I notice some of the aging signs, I am also impressed at Holly's spirit. She doesn't seem to be concerned with age. She still loves to look you right in the eye and demand that you understand what she's thinking.

Report Card: October 1

Emmy Lou:

I notice that she is listed as Emmey-Lou on her medicine container. Is that the correct spelling and have I been insulting her by spelling her name wrong? She doesn't seem to be holding it against me.

Emmy is usually right at my heels when we go out. There were a couple of times when she seemed to get disoriented and headed off in the wrong direction and it was hard to get her attention. With age is she losing some hearing? Or is she just using her age to her advantage?

She is just as cute as always. Emmy took her

medicine very nicely. As you said, the cheese was a treat and I don't think she noticed the pill. We finished off the pills that were in the container. I didn't notice that she was uncomfortable.

Molly Brown:

Molly really looks like she is maturing very nicely. She looks so lovely when she's running. She is beginning to settle down inside for a little longer time before seeing if she can start something and get some action going.

Molly had a nice long time out on Saturday in the kennel. It was windy but not so cold. She was disappointed on Sunday because of the rain. It was cold even when only misting so I did not put her out in the kennel. However, I did try to get her to chase the toy down the hill and bring it back. She gets so excited about earning her treat that I finally discovered that I could save my fingers by tossing the treat in the air for her to catch. This just added another element to our game. She certainly gets focused and hardly ever misses no matter how bad my toss.

Rocky:

Rocky seems to like his new food. He was doing better this time clambering over his rocks. He appears to be very intelligent. He looked at me and I could swear that he understood what I said to him. I find him absolutely amazing!

Report Card October 21

Chewie:

Chewie has such boundless energy and all packaged in such a tiny body. We developed a routine called "Command Performance". I would check his paper while keeping him in the kitchen. If the paper was dirty, I would lay down clean newspaper. Then I would ask him to 'get busy' or 'do his duty' on the clean paper. I would say to him, "We can't go into the other room until you do your business." He would go to the paper and lift his little leg, look up for me to say 'Good Boy' and then head for the gate.

He would stretch his tiny body out on the rug and pull himself across the rug. We spent a lot of time playing, tugging on his toys and tossing them. He is so intelligent. He caught on real fast when I tried to trick him and he would find a way to outsmart me.

He loved the outside. I put his sweater on him because we had such cold days while you were gone. The first time we went out he bounced right out of it. We didn't get out a lot because the weather was also wet as well as cold but we found a few times when the sun came out. He headed right for any mole holes he saw in the ground. The Yorkies were bred to go after rats so I guess he has true breeding in him even if he is mixed with a Poodle.

Each time I left him behind the gate in the kitchen, he would give the most pitiful little cries. He has certainly perfected the ability to work on your pity and guilt. What a little character! Except for that routine, Chewie was delightful and a pleasure to care for.

Report Card: November 8

<u>Molly and Merlin:</u>

When I walked into the house on Friday night, Molly looked so cute. The gate must not have caught when you left, and it was standing open but she was still in the crate. She was practically smiling, like the proverbial cat that swallowed a canary, as she poked her head outside of her crate and looked at me.

Merlin was sitting just outside of Molly's crate facing her. He was keeping her company as he usually did even though her crate was not closed and locked.

They were both very good. However, I sensed that they were a little apprehensive about changes happening in their lives. I reassured them that everything would be okay and that they were still very much loved even if their family is increasing. Two families would be joined in the upcoming wedding and they would just have more people to pet them and spoil them.

Otherwise, things went along normally and well.

House Notes: You sure lost a lot of tree limbs in that storm we had. Molly did a good job of avoiding the ones that would have caught in her chain. I moved a few limbs so we could still run all the way down to the river.

Report Card: November 10

Spike:

Spike was friendly from the very beginning of our first visit. However, he did keep watching for you to come in after me the first couple of times that I visited them. He was welcoming and packed with energy. The weather was good on Friday and especially nice on Saturday. Spike completely surveyed the grounds in the backyard running around the perimeter and up the steps and across the cement wall. He marked his territory as he went. He always kept an eye on me and made sure he knew exactly what I was doing at all times.

Ella:

Ella was shy in the beginning as you said she would be. During the first visit, she stayed pretty much on the stairs and watched me from between the spindles of the banister. If I tried to go to her quietly she would run upstairs. So I just relaxed and didn't pay much attention to her for a while. She soon broke down and came around to be

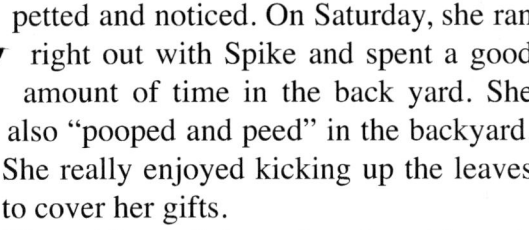

petted and noticed. On Saturday, she ran right out with Spike and spent a good amount of time in the back yard. She also "pooped and peed" in the backyard. She really enjoyed kicking up the leaves to cover her gifts.

House Notes: I cleaned up three big puddles in the dining room. I'm assuming that these were the work of Ella since she wouldn't go outside the first day. It's amazing how much fluid these little ones can hold! 'Accidents' are normal with many dogs (particularly small ones) until they are familiar with me and get over being upset with their masters for leaving them behind. They improved tremendously as they got used to me and found that they could have a good time at home alone or with a stranger.

It was a pleasure being with Spike and Ella. It's amazing how much energy and intelligence is packed into these little 'Yorkie' bodies.

Report Card: November 15

Boots:

Boots has excellent manners. He appeared to greet me when I came in. He walked me to the door when I left. When I put his food down, whether it was dry or wet food, he went right to it and ate some to show how grateful he was.

I brought an embroidery project with me each day to work on after our tasks were done and we were relaxing together. I got quite a bit done early in the week. He would sit on the windowsill or on the couch just above my head. However, as time went on, he wanted more time in my lap. By the last few days, he just totally relaxed in my lap cuddled into my arm. So the sewing just sat on the couch beside us.

One afternoon when I came in, the door to the basement and the litter pan was shut. I'm not sure if I shut it absent mindedly or he did while playing. However, as soon as I went downstairs and opened the door, he raced down the steps and to the litter pan. I did not find any accidents anywhere in the house. He felt so relieved afterwards that he raced around the rooms downstairs for a while. It was the most active that I have ever seen him. He ended up by leaping up on the back of the couch behind where we usually sit together.

Boots has a wonderful temperament, so even-tempered and sweet-natured for a cat.

House Notes: The mail is on the kitchen counter. Also, I found the little plastic pumpkin and the decorative item next to it on the floor under the table nearest the front door. The globe was broken. I think I picked up all of the glass – it had really splintered out. Since Boots was inside all the time he may have tried to peer out at the mailman from the open shelves near the door. Normally, when he was outside more, he probably was used to walking up to him.

Report Card: November 23

Awin:

Awin barked the first night as I came into the house. The second night he barked a little until he heard my voice. By the third night, he already recognized my sound and scent and he didn't bark at all.

First thing each night, we went into the garage and I encouraged him to go through his little door to the fenced in area. Most of the time, he went out and almost immediately came back in. I found it worked really good to put him on the leash and go out to your side yard. We walked around where it was well lighted until he both peed and then pooped. Friday night, he really enjoyed the snow. We took some extra time running around in the snow.

144

He didn't want to come back in but didn't fight me when I insisted. Usually when we came back in, he would spend a little time eating some of his food and milk bones. Thursday night, he really enjoyed chewing on the pig's ear that you left for him. Dogs (and cats) usually eat better when a "human" is around and don't eat as much when left alone.

Awin was very playful. Like a true Jack Russell Terrier, he hardly stopped. We played with different toys, tossing and retrieving. As he got used to me, he became more "cuddly" and would spend some time sitting with me on the couch. As he felt more secure, he would spend a longer time with his "chew bone" (a rubber bone shape filled with dog treats.)

You have done a great job of training Awin. He is definitely a terrier and has his own ideas of what he wants to do but he eventually concedes. He has a good personality: playful with no meanness. When we're playing and he starts to use his teeth, he understands when I say "No teeth!" He quickly gets a toy to play tug with or just to tease me with it. He is smart and resourceful!

Report Card: November 30

Emmy Lou:

Emmy Lou was a very good girl. Only one miss (that I found) in the house! I tried to make sure that she had time to finish her "duty" outside. In spite of her age, she is just as sweet as ever. Every time I tried to get Molly Brown to sit, Emmy would run up and sit for me. She responds so well. The senior food may be helping her. I notice that the older dogs think more clearly after the change in diet.

Molly Brown:

Molly Brown really loved running in the snow. I think she was very disappointed Saturday when the snow melted down and everything was just wet and muddy.

Molly Brown is so beautiful when she gets moving at full speed. I guess it's true that chocolate labs are more hyper active than the black or gold. She definitely needs to run in order to get her bowels moving.

After they both had a chance to relieve themselves, I would let Emmy go back inside while I took Molly Brown to the river and back. I think Molly responds better when she's not in competition for attention.

Following the afternoon run, I left them free in the house until I came back to feed them at night. After our evening visit, they were bedded down in their crates overnight.

Rocky:

Rocky was as intelligent and pleasant as ever. He always comes to the front of the tank to greet the dogs and me when we enter the room to feed him. He still responded to the finger on the side of the tank when I showed him a piece of food that he missed. A couple of times when the food had floated to the other side of the rock, I put my finger in the water and made a current going in the other direction. I think I heard him say, "Thank You!"

Spot:

Spot seemed to like lying on top of the TV when it was on because he got down when I turned it off. Several times he was so comfortable that I left the TV on instead of the radio. It provided them some extra company and he especially liked Pet Planet. Spot seemed to be very serious about his position in the family. He responded with relief when I talked to

him about it and what a good job he is doing. He became very loving and wanted to spend a lot of time in my lap.

Junior:

Junior, as the spoiled young one, seemed to crave a lot of attention. When we played, he had to be reminded that my skin is too thin for teeth and claws. He said, "I only wanted to play and that's the way we cats do it." However, he soon accepted that I would only play with him if he kept his claws in and didn't bite. He has really grown and his very long legs make him taller than Spot. But he is still definitely the "baby" with his high-pitched cry. Spot takes care of Junior, and will step aside for him as an older brother does for a younger one.

Your boys are a wonderful pair and their differences complement each other. They love you very much and feel it's their responsibility to distract you and make you happy.

Hope you had a good Thanksgiving. I have the Thursday and Sunday papers for you. I'll bring them over when I return the key.

Holly:

I came in very late Friday after midnight. Holly didn't bark when I came in but she did keep asking where her pills were. I guess she thought it was morning time. When I did come back later in the morning she was very impatient with me and grabbed the vitamin out of my fingers before I could toss it for her. She remained in charge from that moment on, giving me my orders when she thought the time was right. Often, I would stay longer on the last visit of the evening extending it to two and one-half hours occasionally. One evening when I fell asleep on the couch, she climbed up on the stool, barked at me and licked my face. She said three hours were enough. She demanded to go out to relieve herself and then sent me home.

Holly really seemed to be in good spirits, especially after I told her you emailed me and said that you missed her. Her appetite was good and her movements were regular. We took advantage of Thanksgiving, and I used a tiny bit of "real" (instead of deli) turkey breast with her pills. She had two coughing spells which I was sure were heart related. I just held her chest gently and encouraged her to be calm. When it passed, she was as frisky as ever.

Holly was often very playful. She loved shaking the towel after being wiped down. She demanded that I throw milk bones for her to retrieve, and then wouldn't eat unless I played like I was going to take them from her. I started breaking up a dog biscuit and setting the pieces on the coffee table near where I was sitting. She would come and check. If there were any left, she would bark and demand that I toss one for her. She seemed to have more fun with the pieces than with the whole bisquit.

A few times when I left, I would leave the TV on as a distraction and for company for her while she was alone. I think she seemed more alert and interested. Maybe the TV helped.

House Notes: I had a little trouble with your top lock sticking.

Maybe it happened because of the cold weather. I used some "penetrating oil" on it. It seemed to do the job.

Your driveway was plowed when I came Sunday afternoon.

Report Card: December 8

Turbo:

Turbo seemed to take responsibility for seeing that I prepared meals properly. While Bailey would go into her crate and wait patiently for her food, Turbo seemed to need to keep an eye on me. She watched me carefully as I scooped out the kibble; made sure I put the vitamin in hers and then followed me to the refrigerator to get the can of wet food. Only then was she satisfied that I had not forgotten anything, and returned to her crate waiting for me to finish filling their bowls.

Turbo was most considerate of me when I had them out for their walk. She responded well to the lead and to my voice. The only time I had difficulty with her was when she wanted to go after the men picking up the trash.

Bailey:

Bailey paid me a great compliment when she took one of my shoes and added it to her collection. One night I was late leaving. In fact I might still be there if Bailey had not awakened me where I had fallen asleep in front of the TV. I left my house shoes behind after changing into my snow boots. The next morning one shoe was missing. It was soon located when I checked out Bailey's collection of stolen shoes on her settee.

Bailey was the most solicitous of me while I was in the house. They would both settle down in the kitchen or in their crates, but every so often Bailey would come to me and look in my eyes as if to say, "Is everything okay?" However, she was more determined to follow her own nose outside. I hooked her to the long lead that I had secured on the porch post so that she could take off down the steps without pulling me. Turbo and I could then come down the steps more gently. After they were both off the porch and settled, I would change her to the other lead so we could go for a longer walk.

The cats:

The igloo cats were very interesting. They checked out my truck. I honked my horn when leaving for fear that they might be under the hood for warmth. While none of them came near enough to pet, they seemed to get familiar with my presence and my voice and each day more of them would come out to take a look. Each day, particularly at night I made sure to put out hot water so it would stay unfrozen a little longer. Some of them would come for a drink before it got cold.

General Group Notes:

Each night Turbo and Bailey would follow me into the front room to watch TV. They settled down for a little time and then disappeared. Bailey started staying a little longer. Since they weren't comfortable with me "as family" yet and seemed to stay around the kitchen, I brought some yarn angels to work on at the kitchen table so that I was in the area where they were comfortable. I left my bag of materials on the table, pushed well back and surrounded by mail. However, curiosity gets to dogs as well as cats, and one day my bag was on the floor and well checked out. Not one piece of mail was moved in the process!

That event may have been the turning point of real acceptance. When they saw that I was not pleased but that I still loved them, they followed me into the TV room that night and settled down for a nice long nap. In fact, their snoring kept me awake.

Friday evening I found an empty pill bottle on the kitchen floor. I discovered a turned over trash can in an upstairs' bathroom. I

assumed that one of the dogs found it there. It had been a prescription for Zoloft. (Just in case, I checked with my vet friend for symptoms or side effects. Neither dog was lethargic or hyper.) Sunday morning, at a time when both dogs usually hung around the kitchen I noticed that they had disappeared. I found Turbo lying in the dining room next to her "stash". She had chosen a rug that ran between two rooms as a place to keep her treasures. She had a child's toy, a pillow, a ribbon that she had taken from me, and the pills and bottle cap from the Zoloft. You will find them on the kitchen counter where I placed them. From the number of pills that I picked up, I don't think either dog was interested in them, though it looks like a couple may have had the coating licked off of them.

Since I didn't see the "thief in action", I don't know who got into the pills or where they found them. The empty chewed bottle was near Bailey's settee but it was Turbo who had the other items and 'told me about them'. They both seem unharmed.

House Notes: The Christmas tree was watered (by me, not the dogs). I used the bottle you left on the counter and put a little in each day. Your handyman is very nice. He gets all the credit for bringing up the mail and newspapers. I just brought them inside the house and put them on the table.

Report Card: December 26

Kofi:

Kofi was such a good boy. He greeted me at the door each time I visited him. He would first roll over and ask to be petted. Then he would supervise my activities, watching as I put out his food, washed his dish, refreshed his water, and cleaned his litter pan.

I see what you meant about how he loves the gravy. Before I left in the morning, I would put a little more warm water on the pieces left in his dish. The fluid is probably good for him.

He is certainly regular about eliminating his waste. He seems to be getting too close to the side of his litter pan but he manages to still cover it by scooping out some litter from his pan. So his habits are still "cat clean". However, I find it really easy to pick up because of the newspaper around the pan.

In previous sittings, he used to come in and sit on my lap if I watched TV. However, this time he seemed to like the kitchen better. So I brought some paper work to do at the kitchen table. I didn't get much done because he just had to get up and lie on whatever I was working on. So we had fun 'working around' each other. During these 'close times' I was not able to find anything wrong with his feet that would have caused the bloodstains you had seen previously. He had no trouble getting up and in my way when he wanted to.

Kofi is so cute and still has such a sweet personality. His eyes are always so wide open (a trait that a lot of cats don't have). It makes him look so innocent. I have enjoyed being with him and I'm going to miss seeing him when you move.

Hope you had a good Christmas and best wishes for a wonderful New Year as you find your new retirement home and seek a buyer for your current home!

Report Card: December 26

Pepper:

Pepper really seems to love the snow. She raced for the back door as soon as I came in the house for each visit. When we took our walks – especially on Christmas morning when there was lots of fresh snow and the road was not plowed – she loved to put her nose in the snow and scoop up mouthfuls of it as she walked along. She loved getting into really deep areas to poop – this allowed her to really kick up a storm in her "routine to cover up" and also made it more difficult for me to get to it to pick it up.

She seemed very settled and satisfied. She usually took the lead in starting play. She spent more time just sitting next to me, enjoying being petted and rubbed down. When we went into the TV room, she even got up on the couch with me. (That was a first for me.) She really has a steady temperament even when Sneaky gets a little frisky in play. She is very careful with him.

Sneaky:

Sneaky was a good boy. He greeted me warmly, played hard and spent a lot of time in my lap or lying up against me. He responded well to being touched. You've done a great job of releasing much of his fear. He still lowers his head sometimes as though he's going to be hit. I just rub his little chest gently and reassure him that he will never be hurt again and I can feel him relax.

You were right about the cold and snow bothering his feet. Once the snow started coming, he would do his duty on the porch. I would shovel it up and throw it out into the yard. Christmas was the only time I was a little concerned for him. When it was his turn for a walk in the morning, he ran down to the street and looked in both directions. He saw nothing but snow (since it had not been plowed) so he turned right around and ran back for the door. Since he had peed and pooped on the back porch earlier, it was okay. However, at the late night visit even though I shoveled some open space on the back porch, he couldn't settle down to do anything but just kept scratching at the back door to go back inside and I finally had to let him in. Pepper would have stayed out all night if I had let her.

I was concerned the next morning trying to figure out what to do if he wouldn't do "his duty" outside. However, in the light of day he was fine on the back porch. Since the road was now plowed, he also took a short walk when it was his turn.

We had a great time and we hope you did too!

We had a great time! We are trying to get our parents to go away more often!!

Molly

Emmmmmma

7. The Last Word
The Tails' Turn to Tell Tales

General Consensus: She slept on the job a lot. She called it providing "human presence".

Holly: I even had to wake her up and send her home. **Molly:** I got tired of waiting for my milk bone so I had to remind her to go home. **Jake:** I enjoyed sleeping with her on the couch. **YouYou:** I enjoyed it on the couch with her too. **Boots:** I loved her quietness and her nice soft lap and her gentle arm around me while I slept.

General Consensus: She didn't even ask us what we wanted to watch on TV. **Miasmo:** She did notice that I liked the dog show and put it on again for me.

J.E.B.: She would not be a good trainer. Too easy! But she did respect a person who had trained his/her pets well. **Chances:** I forced her to face her own prejudices like thinking that all Pit Bulls couldn't be trusted. She soon learned that the individual dog and his/her trainer/ guardian was the basis for trust. **Josh:** Well, I was easy to care for but she knew absolutely nothing about my breed until I taught her.

Derry (the invisible cat): She was easy to avoid and hide from. I outfoxed her every time she thought she knew where to find me. **Abdual:** She wasn't afraid to get down on the floor and talk to me under the bed. I liked that. **Dusty:** I wished she would just leave me alone.

Sneaky: She looked cute in "play" position. **Merlin:** I loved trying my de-materializing magic. She really believed that I disappeared. **Beeker:** I hid until she understood that any relationship we were to have had to be on my terms.

Pepper: She got me in trouble. I adjusted to her pace, walking instead of running in the morning. When my family came home, the daughter took me out for a walk. Back at the house she said, "Mother, is something wrong with Pepper? I can't get her to go fast." **Cassie:** My family wasn't too happy when I kept expecting more Chew-eez after they came back home.

Rocky, Lars, Squeaky, Yul: Her experience was so limited having only known dogs, cats and a few birds as family members. We had to teach her that there are many forms of intelligent life capable of bringing joy and love to humans. **Max and Maxine:** Her whistling left something to be desired….it definitely was not "for the birds".

Sadie: I appreciated that she didn't try to force her attention on me but let me decide when (and if) I was ready to accept her
Roger: I taught her the value of "scent" and how an intelligent dog can adjust to so-called "disabilities". There is so much more to life than sight and sound! Attitude makes a big difference. **Harry:** Some of us were just happy to be alive and loved.

Norman: I wish I felt that way! **Bud:** Hey Norman, I had your same disease, and like you I spent most of my time in the basement but she was so good to come and spend time with me there. **Spot:** She was kind when she realized that I was sad sometimes because of the recent death of one of my guardians.

Einstein: It took her long enough to figure out that I was so upset because of my concerns for my guardian when his father was critically ill. She thought the answer to everything was a dog treat!

Mandy and Trixie: We showed her how much fun it is to be with friends who are very different from each other. **Marney:** I tried to be good. She paid attention to me and noticed if I wanted to stay in the yard or come back into the house. **Sarah:** I got her to carry me most of the way to my crate when she was ready to leave by just sweetly lying down and not moving.

All generally agreed: She was so easy to manipulate. All we had to do was to have one little accident in the house, and she would change her schedule to accommodate us, take us outside more often and stay longer for her visits. **Junior:** She was very understanding when I broke the lamp.

Chickadee and Shirley Louise: She sure had a problem with teeth and claws. No patience there!

Been Kitty: Yes, but she was easy to walk over. **Heidi:** I learned how to give her that Beagle look so that she would give me my favorite treat, the ice cream cone without the ice cream. **Puddles:** Well, she didn't take orders very well. All I got was a No.

Ace: It was so easy to snatch up her shoe and tease her to come into the yard barefoot to get it. **Hazel:** She never expected me to grab her sock while resting her feet by the pool but she was a good sport about it. **Bayley:** Well, I think she left her shoes on purpose to see if I would accept her into my family and add her shoe to my stash. **Turbo:** I was smart enough not to eat those nasty pills, but I just liked having variety in my stash. **Emmy Lou:** I preferred stealing milk bones from her pockets.

Moto: I'm glad she had a sense of humor when I turned the house into heaven.

Barn cats: We appreciated her cleverness to put hot water in our bowls so that it didn't freeze up so fast.

Spike, Ella and Chewey: She was a great audience for our fast and bouncy entertainment. She probably enjoyed us little guys because she's so short herself.
Moon, Rosie, and Spooky: She got awfully nervous about our going outside but we knew our way home. We did come in when we would rather stay out just to calm her down. **Molly Brown:** I was glad that she realized how I needed to run outside to release all my energies that built up as I tried to stay quiet inside. **Awin:** Wow! I do know what you mean by "pent up energy". The walks could never be too long.

Gamin: She did seem to respect those of us who have had a longer life experience. **Sebastian:** I noticed that too. But I did make sure that she was reminded when I was ready to be served. **Missy:** She thought I was a little crabby but you know, it's hard to be nice when

there's a big young dog bounding into your territory. **Flopsy:** I agree that a big, active dog in your territory can make you overly nervous and sensitive. **Cinder Cat:** You can say that again. It was good to have a basement hideaway to run to when the chase was on! **Schnitzel:** The top of the book case worked for me to avoid the big dog, but I would rather have been on her lap.

No-No Baby: For those of us who were younger though, she took seriously her responsibility to shake the "devil" out of us. Even so, I enjoyed swinging through the air in her arms. **Iggy:** I would have enjoyed that attention myself but instead I had to create attention-getting activities.

Akeem: I was tough but she made me feel beautiful when she called me "Liz" after Elizabeth Taylor. **Kofi:** Well, I tried to make her look better by trying to fix her hair and all she did was to complain because I pulled a little.

Pretty Cat: I thought she needed supervision. If I didn't direct her activities she would probably have forgotten what to do next. Maybe, she would even have forgotten us!

General Consensus: It was Halloween all of the time: Trick or Treat? We always got the treat!
      Abby: For hired help, she was okay.

About the Author

Margaret Streitenberger worked as a teacher and an accountant. As an adult she chose to share her home with various animals whom she found to be wise, witty, companionable, intrusive, creative and entertaining. She loved reading stories that included animals, especially if the cat or dog helped to solve a mystery.

Retiring from the corporate world, she started a pet sitting business and joined NAPPS (National Association for Professional Pet Sitters) to learn more about the care of pets and meet other professionals in the business. Margaret became a "Tumbleweed" around 2005 and now lives full time with 6 cats and 2 dogs in their motor home.

Margaret can be reached at: tumbleweeds@tailsandtales.com

About the Illustrator

Jim Arnold has been drawing for as long as he can remember. He graduated from SUNY Oswego in 2006, a studio art major and psychology minor. He has always enjoyed animation, illustration, and film. His heroes include Jim Henson, Bill Watterson, and Laurel and Hardy. His work is highly influenced by classic theatrical animated shorts from the early to mid 1900's. Jim lives among 3 cats, 1 dog and 2 horses. He is definitely a cat person – he doesn't know what it's like to live without one.

Jim can be reached at: jimarnold@tailsandtales.com